Born to Stand Out

Tips to Becoming an *Excellent* Computer Consultant

First Edition

published by

Independent
Computer
Consultants
Association

edited by

Bonnie D. Huval

Table of Contents

Foreword

Bookstores have no shortage of books about how to get started as a consultant. Some books even tell how to start in computer consulting.

But then what? If you have appropriate skills and start your practice on the right footing, you can start up just fine—but you find yourself just another ordinary fish in a big sea. This book is about how to become extraordinary.

Many years ago, I noticed three levels of people working alongside me as "outside expertise" on projects. Many do strictly technical work. They are programmers, database administrators, software analysts, any kind of technical specialty. The next level are computer consultants who deal with more than just the information technology aspects of technically oriented projects.

Those are valuable people. But I wanted to join the topmost tier. Although that top level also call themselves computer consultants, they operate in an entirely different league. If a business really needs to raise its game, these elite people are the ones to call.

I found them in the Independent Computer Consultants Association. I joined so I could learn from the best.

Now you can learn from some of the best, too. ICCA was always generous about sharing what its members know. For anyone with a burning desire to be one of the best in this profession, there has never been a better group of teachers and mentors.

Unfortunately, after a third of a century, ICCA dissolved at the end of 2009. To keep this book available, it has been transferred to me as editor. References to ICCA remain undisturbed, except in the "About ICCA" afterword. I hope a successor organization will arise to provide a similar guiding light..

Bonnie D. Huval

Legal Notice

Where anecdotes and examples are given, if the names of businesses other than our own and persons other than ourselves appear inside quotation marks the first time they are used, that means names have been changed to protect privacy. Where actual names are used, the information given can be verified via non-confidential sources such as newspaper archives.

DISCLAIMER: The ideas and suggestions in this book are each contributor's personal opinions. No warranty is expressed or implied. You should not expect any idea here to be applicable to every conceivable type of business. Some ideas or suggestions will fit your situation, but others will not. Also, the contributors are not attorneys, certified public accountants, or licensed insurance agents. No information in this book is intended as complete advice in those areas. Please engage good legal, accounting, and insurance professionals, as appropriate, to help you through those details when you want to implement something from this book. Laws, products available (such as insurance policies), and even accounting practices can vary from place to place or change over time. This book will help you realize what you need. The professionals you engage will guide you toward what is available when you need it.

Computer consulting is among the fields most affected by the fast pace of technological change. Our advice and examples are based on what works as of our publication date. As the future unfolds, please bear in mind that specific tools or media which are ideal for today may be superseded by new tools, media or methods. This book discusses several fundamental principles and philosophies in the computer consulting field, which we hope you will find useful in determining how to make the best use of new developments as they arise.

What Is an Excellent Computer Consultant?

David A. Zimmer, PMP, MCP, CCP (ICCA President)

Bonnie D. Huval (Editor)

In the Information Technology (IT) field, the term "consultant" is not used quite the same way as in most other fields. To become an excellent "computer consultant," first you need to know what it means.

The joke goes something like this: What's a Consultant? It's someone who can't get a real job and carries a briefcase!

Or, it's someone in transition, as in just laid off and in between jobs.

For those of us who are "real" consultants, these jokes are particularly bad because, as we endeavor to provide value-added services to our clients, our clients don't understand the difference between the Real McCoy and the Wannabe Clan.

On the other side of the coin, potential clients are confused by the terms "computer consultant" (which we generally use in this book) or "IT consultant." Frankly, we as an industry have done little to dispel the confusion. Because of the duality of our brand of consulting—both technical and business focused—customers have a hard time understanding who we are and what we do. As excellent computer consultants, we need to help our prospects and current clients overcome the perplexity.

To fully understand how to be excellent computer consultants, we must

- Define consulting in clear terms to clients

- Understand how IT consulting aligns with and differs from the standard definition

- Differentiate between IT consulting and IT contracting, and finally

- Determine who qualifies as an IT consultant, who is an IT contractor, and who is from the Wannabe Clan.

Definition of Consulting

Let's start by defining *consulting*. According to *Answers.com*, consulting is

Consult:

1. To seek advice or information of.

2. To take into account; consider.

3. To exchange views; confer.

4. To work or serve as a consultant.

And again, according to *Answers.com*:

Consultant:

1. One who gives expert or professional advice.

2. One who consults another.

To further understand, let's define two key terms from the above definitions from the same source:

Expert:

1. Person with a high degree of skill in or knowledge of a certain subject.

2. The highest grade that can be achieved in marksmanship.

3. A person who has achieved this grade.

Professional:

1. Of, relating to, engaged in, or suitable for a profession.

2. Conforming to the standards of a profession: professional behavior.

3. Engaging in a given activity as a source of livelihood or as a career.

4. Performed by persons receiving pay.

5. Having or showing great skill; expert.

Putting all of this together, a consultant is a person with a high degree of skill in or knowledge of a certain subject, suitable for his or her profession giving advice as a source of livelihood or as a career.

We can apply this definition to several industries. For example, financial consultants help individuals and companies develop and understand investment strategies, financial market trends and economic impacts to future liquidity. Construction consultants advise on building standards based upon local codes, best practices for particular situations and modern materials best suited for a specific building. Geological consultants help oil companies drill in lucrative oil producing areas instead of areas with no reserves. Management consultants provide information and insight into business situations along with advice to navigate through them to a successful conclusion.

These consultants provide information, knowledge, experience and expertise in a particular field. Normally they don't actually do the work of drilling, construction, mining, etc. They work alongside the client to guide the implementation of recommendations, overseeing progress and suggesting course corrections.

How Computer Consulting Differs From Other Consulting

Some computer consultants work similarly. Others supply hands-on implementation services after recommendations are made. A third group offers staff augmentation services—work similar to that of a client's employees, but on a contract basis. All provide their services under the umbrella of "computer consulting."

To further complicate the matter, we supply both technical consulting and business consulting with a technical flavor. Consequently, when we use the term "computer consultant," people don't know which of the combinations we mean. We may provide multiple combinations to some clients. We can ascertain a business problem, recommend several solutions, implement the chosen solutions, and augment the client's staff for ongoing support.

What self-respecting computer consultant doesn't feel he or she is an excellent consultant with expert knowledge, expertise and skill? Is there a "standard" measure to determine the level of excellence? Is the consultant technical, business, both, specialized, generalized, or what? How does the client know the type of computer consultant and level of excellence needed, let alone recognize the right one?

Contrasting the Wannabe Clan with Genuine Consultants

In a wonderfully written article, *Are You a Real or Imitation Consultant*[1], Aldonna Ambler dispersed the smoke around Wannabe consultants. She worked with a client who became shocked at the number of people who called themselves consultants, but were not. Ambler listed some characteristics of the Wannabe Clan. We've started with her list and added what should be done to become an excellent computer consultant.

- Wannabes expect work to be handed to them. To become excellent, you learn how to find work or determine what needs to be done.

- Wannabes lack the higher education for their topical area. Instead, you develop the habit of continual learning through research, reading, experimenting and if nothing else, establishing a network of knowledgeable peers.

- Wannabes believe the latest presentation at a conference gives them all the knowledge they need. You support your learning at conferences with additional learning to gain higher knowledge.

- Wannabes don't implement their own advice in their practices. You live up to your own words.

- Wannabes think they know what they need to know. Technology is constantly changing. What was important last year is passé this year. You continue learning.

- Wannabes have their favorite solutions. You understand other solutions exist and keep your mind open to additional ways that may be better in a given set of circumstances.

---

[1] Ambler, Aldonna, CMC, CSP. "Are You a Real or Imitation Consultant." Speaker, the professional speakers' magazine from the National Speakers Association (NSA), May 2006.

- Wannabes lack facilitation and project management skills. Clients want solutions and management of those solutions. Clients want to feel secure that their interests are more important than the Wannabe's. You learn how to break complex situations into smaller, simpler, more manageable pieces. You are able to manage projects and facilitate in complex situations. You develop "people skills," not just skills with technology.

- Wannabes have never learned how to provide advice. You are able to pinpoint problems and recommend options from which the client may choose without making the client feel like you "led the witness" to the your personal favorite choice.

- Wannabes lack credibility and demonstrated success. You establish credibility through referrals, publishing, research and other methods.

- Wannabes lack depth and breadth of experience. We all lack experience at the beginning of our careers, but Wannabes stay there. As you progress in your consulting, you orchestrate your collection of experience to build breadth and depth, and portray it appropriately.

One final trait of Wannabes deserves to be singled out as perhaps the most important: They have not fully decided whether they want to be a consultant or will simply masquerade as one until a "real" job comes along. As a result, they are not fully committed. To transition from Wannabe to Consultant, you make the commitment and take steps to become a genuine Consultant.

From Genuine Consultant to Excellent Consultant

To transition from an average consultant to excellence, consultants must continue with learning and study.

In his book "Break From The Pack,"[2] Oren Harari discusses commoditization of almost any business. He states those companies who once had market-leading products and services eventually saw them become commodities sold on price rather than value. Competitors saw the leader's success, copied it and drove the market to shop by comparing prices rather than picking the original.

---

[2] Harari, Oren. "Break From the Pack: How to Compete in a Copycat Economy." FT Press, September 3, 2006.

Kleenex® is a clear example of this phenomenon. Once the biggest player in the facial tissue market, Kleenex®, a Kimberly-Clark Worldwide registered trademark, has become the common name for facial tissue and consumers often buy the cheaper competitors.

DuPont™ offers other examples, having lost the trademark to the name "nylon" to common usage, and inspired follow-on competitors offering products similar to inventions such as Kevlar®.

Although Harari's book slants more to products and services for general consumers, computer consulting services are not immune to commoditization. Harari postulates the solution for such a transition is to stay ahead of the pack by developing "the next level." Those who stay in the middle of the pack become invisible and must compete on price.

Excellent consultants constantly strive toward the next level of knowledge, skill, expertise, and experience. They enlarge their boundaries, advance the industry and lead the market to where it wants to go.

At the same time, this does not necessarily mean they work only with the leading edge. Their breadth allows them to apply the *right* solutions for each client, which may be leading edge, mature technology, or a blend of old and new technology. Such wisdom is not possible from longtime practitioners who do not keep up with advances in the field, or from comparative newcomers who were taught with technologies which are currently most popular and have not yet had a chance to learn more.

Going back to familiar products for an example, one of the most successful aramid fibers competing against Kevlar® sold well for bullet resistant body armor vests. When new, it is stronger, so vests can be made lighter and with less of the expensive fiber. However, it deteriorated over time more quickly than Kevlar®. Some vests failed unexpectedly early, a highly undesirable trait in a life-protecting product. This led some large purchasers, including government agencies, to demand Kevlar® even if it costs more. Investment by DuPont™ in the quality of its product pushed back against commoditization.

The best computer consultants invest regularly in both updating and broadening their expertise to make certain they continue to deliver high quality advice and expertise in a changing world.

So What Is A Computer Consultant Anyway?

The title "consultant" has a certain air, panache, mystic, and finesse that "contractor" or "wannabe" do not. Of course, all of us who sell our services to clients want to be known as consultants. From our list above, we can tell whether we deserve the title.

But that leaves clients with a dilemma. How can they distinguish the Real McCoy from the Wannabe? When customers hire outside expertise, they don't want a smoke-n-mirrors show that leaves them drained of money, time, and emotion. They want return on their investment—true, tangible return.

Unfortunately, in the IT industry, some people use the term "contractor" and "consultant" interchangeably. Are they the same? Can they do similar work and have the same qualifications? Or are they really different?

What Technical Contract Workers Do

Technical contract workers apply technical skills which are their specialty. Customers determine what needs to be accomplished, contract with an IT specialist in the area of need, and let the contractor do the work.

For example, a software designer is told what the software has to do. A contract programmer writes the code to meet specifications provided by the client.

Good contractors are self-starters with excellent technical skill and produce superb technical work with less need for supervision and motivation than most regular employees. After completing the project, contractors leave without fuss. Whatever the project built is left for employees to maintain.

Contractors can be used for staff augmentation, either filling voids in headcount without permanency or providing specialty skills needed only for a limited period of time. Their scope of work is defined by the client. While a contractor may see additional areas for improvement or work, the scope of work is constrained to the task at hand.

Contract technical workers do exclusively technical work. One contract programmer stated outright that he would only write software to do what the software specifications said. He did not want to pay attention to anything else. He didn't care to learn what equipment ought to do in response to commands sent by his software. He especially wanted not to deal with people to learn what they wanted. He wrote good software and focused on it exclusively.

A good contract technical worker is extremely valuable for the right technical task. Teaming up a top computer consultant with some top contractors for implementation can be highly effective. But if the contractor begins to claim to be a consultant without an appropriate expansion of scope, perspective and skills, the contractor joins the Wannabe Clan.

What Computer Consultants Do

Typically, computer consultants begin as technical workers. The consultant develops some expert technical skills (designing, programming, testing, networking, and so on) and develops a wide swath of the skills needed for the entire birth, life and eventual death of a system. But the consultant's professional growth goes beyond adding and polishing technical skills.

The recipe for a computer consultant looks like this: Begin with computer capability. Add hefty doses of business acumen, common sense, and "soft skills." Bake in the oven of experience and out pops a computer consultant.

To become an excellent computer consultant, continue to add ingredients of experience, learning, discovery, research, credentials, and bake on high and test by fire. Repeat this process regularly.

The primary difference between a contractor and a consultant is the consultant's view of the contract. Whereas the contractor is hired for a specific aspect of a project, the consultant ascertains the big picture, ties actions to business initiatives, recommends technical solutions appropriately and always works in the best interest of the client regardless of the impact to the consultant.

Characteristics of an Excellent Computer Consultant

In the article by Ambler, she developed a list for consultants. Again, we embellish her list:

A real consultant is expected to:

- bring appropriate credentials to a situation that result in *expanded information* and *knowledge*

- bring *objectivity* to a situation

- bring *innovative thinking* to a situation

- bring *facilitation skills* to a situation

- adhere to a *professional code of ethics*

- have a *continual learning* and *self-improvement* process

- *work in the best interest* of the *client.*

Let's expand on these ideas so we understand what they really mean.

Credentials

The consultant should have appropriate credentials. Credentials come in different forms: educational, designations, research, practical knowledge and experience, and previous successes (and failures—a real consultant learns from failure so clients don't experience those failures).

As a consultant, do you possess an advanced degree? Lest you think we are snobs, we do realize years of experience can equate to formal education. However, in advanced degrees, students are taught more in-depth information and also learn advanced ways of thinking and research.

Although there are many bright people without advanced degrees who run circles around those with degrees, an advanced degree shows a level of commitment and dedication to a particular topic. Additionally, it represents a simple validation for the client of authenticity, knowledge and dedication.

Aside from formal education, further study or published research shows potential customers ongoing improvements. Customers want to know a consultant's education didn't stop after the diploma. Otherwise, the consultant's education and information becomes stale very quickly, especially in the fast-paced world of IT.

Objectivity

A consultant's information must be unbiased. Clients want to know why a consultant recommends a particular solution. Is it because of their favorable experience with said product or service, or because they receive financial restitution? Clients want unbiased, non-directed information. A consultant helps clients make informed decisions that align with business goals and objectives. As consultants, we must not give allegiance to a particular vendor or supplier. The consultant should walk into a client's site with a clean slate as to any products or services that would fit the customer's needs.

This does not mean consultants should not know or understand the values of many various competing products or services. They should clearly know the available set of solutions for the client's situation. But the needs analysis derived from discovery should drive the consultant's recommendation. While the consultant might have a favorite solution, he/she should willingly set favoritism aside to recommend the solution best suited for the client's needs.

When the consultant may receive any type of compensation if the client purchases the consultant's recommendation, an ethical consultant clearly lets the client know such compensation may occur. Again, the consultant must not let that potential compensation mar or influence his or her recommendation.

Facilitation Skills

Facilitation is a fancy word for "make easy," "make possible," and "smooth the progress of." Excellent consultants aren't just technically savvy in their area of technical expertise, but know other skills to get the job done. More importantly, they know how to put ownership of the project back into the hands of the client and not keep it to themselves, so the client is not left at their mercy.

One of us just got off the phone with a colleague who is trying to get a client back online with their small business server. The situation is dire because the server is not working properly due to multiple Trojan viruses, worms, and other viruses—and those are the simple problems.

The real problems are a result of a "high powered consultant" (and we are using those terms very loosely here) who originally configured the machine. That "consultant":

- used improperly licensed software (translation: illegal) to create the server

- illegally hosted websites on the server at the client's expense and for the consultant's gain

- registered the company's domain address in such a way that only the consultant can configure the domain records

- established several backdoor accounts with secret passwords in case the client changes the main password, and

- a slew of other major and unethical offenses.

Who knows what other data and information the consultant used to his advantage? Now the consultant has moved on to other grounds and left the client in the lurch.

To top all this off, the client is upset because the machine no longer functions properly. The client blames our colleague for the malfunctioning, even though the machine was not working properly before he came aboard (which is why the client called for a new consultant in the first place)! Yet the client stands firmly behind the expertise of the schlock consultant.

At the least, facilitation requires a five-step methodology:

- problem/opportunity identification

- research

- design

- implementation

- evaluation (evaluation may identify something that requires another iteration of this process for continued improvement)

A Real McCoy consultant knows how to manage this process and move the client forward with tangible deliverables and results.

Notice, the actual root of the trouble in our example is not technical, it's human. That adds an entire layer to facilitation—and excellent computer consultants always pay attention to that human layer. A top computer consultant often spends more time and energy on the human side than on the technical side. The engagement is a relationship, not just a sale, with the client.

Professional Code of Ethics

As excellent computer consultants, we hold ourselves to a higher standard than those who have not committed to consulting. We subscribe to acting in the best interest of our clients, providing top quality and ethical service. We do not engage in unscrupulous behavior. We do not use improper, illegal, or unethical practices, even when money sits on the table for the taking. Our reputation is more important than any amount of money and we protect our integrity above all else. Not everyone has their price—some are priceless.

As real consultants, we do not simply have a business license and worker's compensation insurance. We carry the insurance coverage, accreditation, certifications and licenses necessary to ply our trade. We continue to grow our knowledge and skills through formal education, providing our clients with the latest information and expertise.

We put our clients first. Pure and simple.

To some, this may sound idealistic, but not realistic. The fact of the matter is that many consultants do hold to these values. Sadly, there are also many that do not. Our clients must determine who are the Real McCoys and who are the Wannabes, the ethical consultants and the unethical. Our job is to make it simple to distinguish us from the Wannabe Clan. This book provides tips to help you do that and be an excellent consultant.

If you've committed yourself to consulting, you were "Born To Stand Out." Follow these tips and do it.

Conclusion

Excellent consultants are not born ready to step into our roles. We are born with the drive to stand out. Then we are crafted over time following logical, rational steps to continually improve ourselves, our knowledge and our craft. We possess savvy technical skills, smart business focus, and a keen eye for results that benefit the client. Our combination of business acumen and technical knowledge ensures clients use the appropriate technology to meet business objectives.

This book is dedicated to advancing the industry of computer consulting. The Independent Computer Consultants Association (ICCA at **www.*icca*.org**) has been the driving force for the industry over thirty-three years. Founded in 1976 to fulfill the need by independent consultants and clients alike to establish ground rules and excellence standards, ICCA continues to advance the industry through education.

ICCA requires members to sign and abide by its professional code of ethics (included at the end of this book). It informs members of legislative and other mandatory issues regarding new legal requirements as they occur.

This book is the first of a planned series serving top tier computer consultants and their clients.

Three Questions for Starting a New Assignment

Gerald "Jerry" M. Weinberg

Jerry writes "nerd novels," such as "The Aremac Project" and "Mistress of Molecules," about how brilliant people produce quality work. More of his novels may be found as eBooks at

www.geraldmweinberg.com/Site/eBooks.html

Before taking up his science fiction career, he published books on human behavior, including "Weinberg on Writing: The Fieldstone Method," "The Psychology of Computer Programming," "Perfect Software and Other Fallacies," and an "Introduction to General Systems Thinking." He also wrote books on leadership including "Becoming a Technical Leader," "The Secrets of Consulting" (foreword by Virginia Satir), "More Secrets of Consulting," and the four-volume Quality Software Management series. He incorporates his knowledge of science, engineering, and human behavior into all of writing and consulting work (with writers, high-tech researchers, and software engineers).

Early in his career, he was the architect for the Mercury Project's space tracking network and designer of the world's first multiprogrammed operating system. Winner of the Warnier Prize and the Stevens Award for his writing on software quality, he is also a charter member of the Computing Hall of Fame in San Diego and the University of Nebraska Hall of Fame. His website and blogs may be found at **www.geraldmweinberg.com**.

The idea for this article came from a student in my Problem Solving Leadership workshop. I taught these three questions, and he found them so useful he thought I should write them for others to read "because you (Jerry) look at the business of contracting and consulting and the people skills involved, which translate across all skill sets and even industries"—in other words, the big picture.

That's flattering, isn't it? But wait a minute! Why would you want to look at the Big Picture? If you're like me, you're often called into an assignment because you're supposed to be an "expert." You know what an expert is: "someone who avoids all the small mistakes while committing a grand blunder." So, before I get down to the nitty-gritty of a new assignment, I like to place everything in a grand array. I always make mistakes in my assignments, but this way I can hope they'll all be small mistakes.

My favorite method of approaching the Big Picture is first to break down the question into three parts: Self, Other, and Context. In this chapter, I'll start with Self—that is, the Big Picture of yourself.

Focusing on myself, I then ask the three questions I learned from the famous family therapist, Virginia Satir:

- How do I happen to be here? (Past)

- How do I feel about being here? (Present)

- What would I like to have happen? (Future)

The Big Picture of Myself

How do I happen to be here?

- If it's the first assignment with this client, how did I make the connection? Was it through a third party, or through a direct contact by the client?

- If it's a repeat, what impressions did I leave the previous times I was here? Did I leave friends? Enemies? Are my old contacts still viable? What assumptions am I carrying over from the previous assignments?

- Did I get the contract I wanted, or did I have to make some concessions that might come back to haunt me?

How do I feel about being here?

- Am I here reluctantly? Do I have some reservations, or forebodings, about this assignment?

- Am I eager to be here? Am I looking forward to the task I've agreed to do?

- Am I puzzled about what's expected of me, or is the assignment clear? How sure am I of the assignment?

- How sure am I of myself—of my ability to provide value for value received?

- However I'm feeling, is this the right mood for succeeding in this job? If not, what steps will I have to take to get in the right mood?

What would I like to have happen?

- Why did I take this assignment? For the money? The experience? The challenge? The possibility of a future reference? If I don't have my mission in mind whenever I choose a course of action, the client might be happy with my work, but I'll come away with a hollow feeling.

- What will success look like, to me? If I come away with a pile of money but a poor reference, will I be satisfied? How about an ecstatic client who's enormously impressed by my repeating a solution I've done so often it bores me into a trance?

- How long do I want to be here? If the client wants to extend the project, will I be laughing or crying?

Using the Big Picture of Yourself

By using these three questions to assess my own state before I start an assignment, I've enormously increased my level of satisfaction. I use them to survey my state before I agree to any contract, new or renewed. On one occasion, for instance, I found I was about to renew a long-standing contract with a nice 15% increase in my daily fee. When I checked my feeling, however, I realized that I had negotiated for the wrong thing. Much of the time on the old contract, I felt that I was doing a fine job in solving the wrong problem, and I don't find this situation highly satisfying. I didn't mind the extra 15%, but what I really wanted was more involvement in defining my own assignments.

Armed with improved self-knowledge, I halted the negotiation process and asked for more leeway, which the client was only too happy to grant. I was prepared to sacrifice at least some of the 15% increase, but the client insisted that I take it. He commented, "Now that you'll be helping do the right things, rather than just doing things right, you'll be worth at least that much more to us."

Self-assessment doesn't always pay off this directly. On another renewal, early in my career, my attempt to get more leeway in defining my work led to an irreconcilable difference between me and my client. This client knew—or thought he did—exactly what his problems were, yet I felt his inadequate problem definition limited my ability to be successful in my terms.

At that time in my life, what I wanted most was to gain experience with certain types of problems and perhaps come away with a few outstanding references. On my first assignment with this client, I had helped solve a problem that didn't vaguely resemble what I really wanted to work on. Although the solution was innovative and successful, it didn't really help the client with her true problem since she was working on the wrong problem to begin with. She attributed her lack of satisfaction to some unspecified shortcoming in my work, and was reluctant to give me a sterling reference.

Of course, she was right. The shortcoming in my work was my failure to assess the Big Picture—both hers and mine—before I took the assignment. As we negotiated for a follow-on, the three questions showed me that the extra money she offered wasn't adequate to overcome my bad feelings about working with her again. Negotiations broke down, but at least I didn't waste another six months of my life struggling for something I didn't really want.

It took me a few weeks to obtain a new assignment, and that cost me a few bucks. The cost is long forgotten, but I still savor the memory of my satisfaction with the new assignment—what I learned, what I earned, and how it put my professional life back on my own track.

Seeing the Other Person's Big Picture

You're entering a new situation, and you're ready to gather the Big Picture of the other people involved. Whatever you do, don't try the following process without first getting a Big Picture of yourself. If you're not personally centered, this whole process will sound hollow and even smarmy.

Which others' Big Pictures? Well, who will the significant others be? Anybody I omit from this survey will potentially appear on stage at a critical juncture and spoil my best laid plans. The people I usually have to consider are Dani, my wife and business partner; Caro and Lovey, my German Shepherd dogs and biggest supporters; Lois and Susie, my coworkers; other colleagues in my network, such as my PSL and AYE faculty colleagues; my customer, the one who's going to pay my bills. For this chapter, I'll focus on the example of my clients, the ones I'm going to work with on this assignment.

I'll look for the answers to the three Big Picture questions:

- How do *they* happen to be here? (Past)

- How do *they* feel about being here? (Present)

- What would *they* like to have happen? (Future)

Let's see how these questions help me get off on the right foot, even when presented with a bad beginning.

Soon after I arrived at her organization, my client Darlene volunteered, "We've had consultants before, but none of them made any difference." Darlene's remark is one I've heard before, and used to put me on the defensive. Now, however, I simply ask myself, "What does this mean, and what should I do about it? Let's see how the three questions can help me."

How do they happen to be here? (Past)

When someone talks about past consultants, they've given me a free head start without making me ask one of my "past" questions, such as:

- Did Darlene choose to be here, or was she forced by me, or some other factor, like her boss?

- What has been her past history on this job? What knowledge does she have that I can tap into? What prejudgments has she made about the nature of this task?

- Has she had early personal or cultural experiences that might affect they way she works on this job? With me? These are not excuses for poor performance, but things I have to understand to work well with Darlene.

- What's been her past experience with me? With other contractors? What preconceptions does she bring to the table as a result of these experiences?

How do they feel about being here? (Present)

In this instance, I knew right away that this organization "had consultants before, but none of them made any difference." Obviously, Darlene felt that this was an important thing to say, but I didn't know why she brought this up so early in our relationship:

- Does she have some reservations, or forebodings, about this assignment? About me? Does our doing this assignment conflict with something else she wants to do?

- Is she eager to be here? Is she looking forward to working with me on the task that I've agreed to do?

- Is she clear about what's going to be required of her if I take this assignment?

- How's her self-esteem? Does she feel able to control her situation and accomplish her personal goals, or does she feel powerless?

- However she's feeling, is her mood the right mood for me to succeed in this job? If not, what steps can I take to help her get into the right mood?

I often seek this information by asking, "And what does that tell you about my tour of duty?" Here are some of the answers I've received from Darlene and other people, at other times:

- Aaron: "You don't have a chance, so I'm not going to waste any time helping you."

- Bonnie: "You're going to need my help if it's going to turn out differently this time."

- Carter: "It's nothing personal, but this will be another of those management vision things, full of sound and fury and going nowhere."

- Darlene: "I'm really excited, because you're different from any of the consultants we've had before. This time, our consultant is really going to make things better around here."

Each of these answers is full of information, but I'm going to work differently with each of these people.

What would they like to have happen? (Future)

First, though, I have to know the answer to the third question, "What would you like to have happen?"

- Why did X agree to work with me on this assignment? Is it the experience? The challenge? Fear of the boss?

- What will success look like, to X? Is it aligned with my own success criteria? Did previous consultants solve problems that X failed to solve, thus making X look like a failure?

- How long does X want me to be on this assignment? Will I be able to stay long enough to see it through? If the customer extends the project, will X be laughing or crying?

My Responses

Assuming each of them genuinely hoped something would change but knowing that each felt differently about my being here, I would construct different responses, perhaps as follows:

- to Aaron: ["You don't have a chance, so I'm not going to waste any time helping you."] "I can understand your feeling, Aaron. I'll do my best not to waste any of your time, but if I should happen to come up with something that might save you some time, would you be interested in hearing about it?"

- to Bonnie: ["You're going to need my help if it's going to turn out differently this time."] "Great! What sort of help do you think you can give me?"

- to Carter: ["It's nothing personal, but this will be another of those management vision things, full of sound and fury and going nowhere."] "Yes, I've sure seen my share of futile, grandiose projects. I personally think that big changes result from an accumulation of small changes. Would you be willing to work with me on some small thing that would help you in some way? Then we could see if we're wasting our time, or if things might be different this time."

- to Darlene: ["I'm really excited, because you're different from any of the consultants we've had before. This time, our consultant is really going to make things better around here."] "I'm flattered. Thank you. In what way do you think I'm different from the others, and why do you think that will help?"

As a result of learning their Big Picture, I'm no longer knocked off balance. Instead, I'm well centered and already beginning to create a method of working appropriately with each of my client's people.

Question and Answer

Q: How do you come up with such responses in real time? They make sense when I read them, but in the moment, I often go blank.

A: There's a pattern, but it won't work if you think it's a formula. You must remain creative in order to fill in the pattern, so the first thing you must always do is center yourself. Then, find a way to connect with the emotional content of what they're saying, relating your own emotional state to theirs. Only then can you proceed to the content—what they want to have happen, and you might do next to move toward what they want.

Q: It's all very nice to say that I ought to be centered in myself before I make big decisions, but whenever I get into some sort of negotiation, I lose track of myself, what I want, and what's good for me. What do you suggest?

A: This is too big a question to answer entirely, but the first part is easy. When you first notice that you're starting to lose yourself, STOP whatever you're doing. Then concentrate on how you're breathing, and switch to smooth, regular breathing. I could write a book on the following parts—in fact, I have. (See my book "Quality Software Management: Volume 3: Congruent Action."[3].)

Q: I've tried the breathing thing, and sometimes it works. But sometimes it doesn't, like when another person is blasting at me in a loud voice. What should I do?

A: If you can't get your breathing under control, find a way to leave the situation. If you wish to continue, come back later. If you find yourself unable to leave, then that's a sure sign you must leave, now—and not come back. This is not the situation for you.

---

[3] Weinberg, Gerald M. "Quality Software Management: Volume 3: Congruent Action." 4 vols. Vol. 3. New York: Dorset House, 1994.

The Power of "Business-Speak"

Jason Harrison

Jason is founder and president of Harrison Technology Consulting. Established nearly 20 years ago with a focus on helping small to medium-sized businesses (SMBs) get the most out of their technology investments, Harrison Technology Consulting has emerged as a thought leader and visionary in the SMB technology consulting market.

Over the years Jason has been a contributing writer to a number of SMB focused business publications, a regular speaker at SMB focused technology events, a past speaker at a number of Microsoft® Worldwide Partner Conferences, and a regular contributor and speaker at SMB focused technology user groups. He has also co-authored several technical whitepapers on various different SMB focused technology solutions.

Jason was one of the early pioneers in expanding his technology consulting firm's impact via managed services. As early as 1995, Harrison Tech began offering managed services to its clients to help SMBs deal with the changing face of technology in a more efficient, predictable, and effective way.

With a strong business process focus tied to solid infrastructure best practices, Jason has consistently delivered solid business technology solutions to his clients for nearly two decades. In addition, Jason has provided consulting services to a number of company's product development divisions, helping them deliver the right solutions for the SMB market.

To learn more about Jason and Harrison Technology Consulting, visit **www.harrisontechconsulting.com**.

As an independent technology consultant, you are expected to be highly knowledgeable in whatever technical areas of expertise you have chosen for your concentration. Depending on the market you serve, you must also have varying degrees of business acumen to help fit the technology into the business model and processes already in place. You may also help streamline and redefine those processes as a result of the impact of the technology being introduced.

This chapter takes a look at various markets and how the level of business skill needed can vary. You will also discover the often overlooked impact that a strong "business-speak" skill set can have on your ability to deliver technology solutions that hit home for your clients. The term *business-speak* is used throughout this chapter to define overall business acumen, skill, and the ability to "speak the language" at the appropriate level.

Let's begin by examining some markets and the required business-speak levels that are unique to each. This is an executive overview of these markets with several generalizations. Some specifics and variations will not be addressed here. The purpose is to simply construct a basic definition and understanding.

Variations in Relation to Client Size

In the enterprise and mid-to-upper-mid-market, a typical technology consultant can be very specialized and have a high degree of focus on a specific technology or technology area. For example: a consultant may specialize in certain database technologies. Oddly enough, the overall level of business-speak needed can vary, since business process consultants or specialists usually represent the business side of a given project. Knowing business terminology helps greatly in these scenarios. Often the business jargon and terminology at this level are much more extensive than in smaller organizations. The need to communicate and understand business-speak at a higher level is prevalent; however, you are less likely to need to fill missing gaps in business acumen to execute your role in the project. Stronger, more deeply focused technology skill sets tend to prevail at this level.

When you step farther down into the lower-mid market and the SMB space (Small to Medium-sized Business, where I am deeply rooted), several factors demand broader business acumen. The leading factor is that typically fewer of the people involved have both a technology and business background. There are also fewer people who fully understand the technology side and how it all fits together. Often the computer consultant must fill business knowledge gaps, or even introduce new business-speak concepts and processes, throughout the project's duration.

Technology projects tend to cross a broader section of the company in this market segment. SMB technology projects usually affect the core fabric of how the company operates. There are many other side issues as well; however, the above are the major ones I focus on here.

The fact that comprehensive business acumen is needed in the SMB space initially seems counter-intuitive because the business side of SMB is often far simpler than in larger businesses. As soon as you scratch the surface, overall requirements on the technology consultant turn out to be broader and more demanding. You must become a solid generalist in technology as well as business processes and how it all works together to craft an effective end solution.

Computer Consultants with SMB Clients

The main challenge in the SMB market is that the overwhelming majority of technology service providers (consultants, value-added resellers, and so on) are overly focused on the technology side, and don't focus on the real meat and potatoes of how their clients actually use technology solutions to operate their business. I read a report not long ago that said over 80% of SMB consultants and VARs are primarily focused on infrastructure only: servers, workstations, disaster recovery, e-mail, Internet access, security, etc. Most do not get involved with the business processes side: accounting, automated business processing, workflow automation, etc.

Ironically, most tell surveyors they want to develop a more strategic relationship with their clients. They want to become the "trusted advisor" on a par with the CPA or attorney, but in regard to technology strategy for their clients' overall business operations. Until they engage with their clients on the business operations side, it simply will not happen.

The SMB market is ripe for consultants to help clients make better, smarter, more strategic technology decisions in relation to business process automation. It is an underserved market waiting for a solid solution. Why? *Not enough good technology consultants are out there who have strong business acumen and focus on the SMB market segment.*

Many CPA firms only go so far to help end clients with their accounting. They cover the fundamentals, but other elements such as CRM integration, manufacturing management systems, and work flow automation go unaddressed or are left up to SMBs to figure out on their own. There is so much opportunity here, I am amazed that so many technology service providers in the SMB space have not fully caught on yet.

Impact of Having Business Acumen

Regardless of which market segment you work in, having solid business acumen expands your potential to do much more for your clients. How it affects your business is less obvious. Regardless of whether you focus more on being an independent consultant or a hybrid VAR / managed services provider / consulting firm, the benefits your firm can reap are endless.

Whether serving the core SMB space or the enterprise, bringing extensive business acumen to the table means you see everything differently. You recognize details that go unnoticed by others, which allows you to take on opportunities that are invisible to those who lack these skills. It also immediately changes the way your clients perceive you as a professional. When a client sees and understands that you are more than just a technology expert, they treat you differently from the beginning. It becomes much easier to obtain "trusted advisor" status and instantly sets you apart from the average technology consultant.

What *Is* Business-Speak?

So what exactly is business-speak?

It is the ability to perceive, analyze, discuss and address business problems in concert with technology solutions while aligning with the client's overall business objectives. It is the ability to articulate the value of solutions in terms of benefit to the business rather than technical terms. It also encompasses integrating the power of infrastructure with the fundamentals of business process management solutions that directly affect a client's performance and bottom line.

My firm's technology projects usually involve putting infrastructure in place, then building the genuine substance of a solution on top of that infrastructure. The infrastructure (including servers, workstations, network, security) is simply the foundation on which real work is done. In the client's eyes, "real work" appears to be in the tools, technologies, and processes used to actually manage their day-to-day business operations. This can involve a broad set of solutions and technologies, ranging in scope from accounting and other line-of-business solutions to workflow, customer relationship management, and collaboration tools.

Having robust business acumen allows you to see and understand how a client's business operates. Your ability to integrate all the technological and business pieces together to provide a solid solution will earn thanks from your clients time after time.

An owner recently told me, "If it was not for your vision to put the right tools in place for us well before we really needed them, we would not be here." He was referring to the recent economic shift we all have experienced over the last year or so. Our original project put key performance indicators right in front of him daily via a dashboard, so he could easily see the impact the downturn was having on his business. That information allowed him to make quick adjustments that kept his business viable through the rough economic period.

Another example is a small general contracting firm I've worked with over the last few years. After putting their core infrastructure in place, we helped them implement a streamlined and more efficient integrated accounting and job costing solution that has helped them become more profitable per job. As the economic downturn hit, this helped them respond effectively to changes in the market. Again, the right solution kept their business viable in a tough economy.

Because of the positive impact we made on these firms and many similar stories, I know we will have these clients for life. I know that even as other technology solution providers or consultants call on them for their business, these clients will not even consider the competitors. The fact that we were able to apply technology to help their businesses in deeply meaningful ways truly benefited their performance. Ultimately that is what overall business-speak is really all about.

It's About Solving Problems, Not Promoting Technology

Another aspect of business-speak is always approaching clients from a solution perspective rather than a technology-focused perspective. When you hire someone to build a house, do you care about what brand of tools they use to build your home? The same should be true for all technology consultants and solution providers. While the brands you work with to deliver a solution can be important, they should only be secondary. You should always carry out projects with your primary focus on business impact and the business solution. In the end, clients don't care whether you use software from Microsoft®, Intuit®, or Sage®. They don't care whether the hardware comes from Hewlett-Packard®, Dell®, or another brand. As long as the solutions solve their businesses needs, that's what really counts.

As new technologies arrive in various market segments, having an expansive skill set that involves more of a business-oriented focus will help your firm thrive. Just consider the impact that Software as a Service (SaaS) or "cloud computing" will have on certain segments of the market. Cloud computing reduces infrastructure demand at the client's site, but the need for help implementing and integrating technology solutions into their business process flow will remain. Expanding your business acumen will ultimately put your firm ahead of the pack as we begin seeing more and more of a shift in computing paradigms over the next five to ten years.

How to Start Building Your Business-Speak

I recommend starting by getting a firm grasp of accounting fundamentals. This will not only help you with your clients regardless of the industry they are in, but also expand your own ability to better manage your firm's financials.

You also need to focus on specific industries in which you provide service. For example, if you tend to work with manufacturing firms, it makes sense to build your knowledge of manufacturing processes and related business terminology. If you focus on medical firms, you may want to develop a better understanding of related business model requirements, workflows, regulatory requirements, and systems used to manage a medical practice. You don't need a Master's degree in Business Administration, but having some exposure to certain segments of what a typical MBA has learned will go a long way in helping you achieve a higher level of business-speak.

You can obtain much of your business acumen through self-paced learning, adult learning programs at your local college or community college, online business training, and sheer experience as you work with various clients in various industries. I find that I am always learning something new as part of my own personal journey. Often some of the most valuable things I have learned come from working with clients. Even developing best practices in your own firm's operations can help you learn many of the same fundamentals that your clients also face and often need help with.

It is possible to build your business-speak repertoire by hiring it through expanding your staff or partnering with other firms that cover these areas. However, with this approach you will not reap the same benefits as building your own personal knowledge. Being strong in both technical and business acumen is irreplaceable at the end of the day. An individual who has both brings something unique to the table. Combined with a touch of creativity and vision, business-speak can become your secret weapon to ensure your success now and well into the future.

Other chapters in this book delve into ways in which you can develop or expand your skills, and your clients' recognition of them. Of course, no matter how many skills you develop and how well you can speak the language of business, everything revolves around the points made early in this book by Jerry Weinberg: *Keep in mind why you are working with your clients, and pay attention to why they engage you.* In a sense, the most important part of business-speak is not what you say, it's how well you listen, observe, and understand.

Set Yourself Apart as an Expert

Diane Herrera

Diane is the president and founder of CSSI, a software and consulting firm located in King of Prussia, Pennsylvania. CSSI helps investment management firms automate and customize their portfolio management systems. The company specializes in Advent's Axys™ and Schwab's PortfolioCenter™ and other software systems. CSSI has been responsible for the design and implementation of dozens of reporting and packaging systems. Firms that need custom reports, special interfaces, data cleanup, report packages, automation, or back office reconciliation assistance can find a willing and able resource at CSSI. Visit **www.cssi.org** *for more information about CSSI's products and services.*

Diane holds a master's degree in mathematics from Baylor University. She served as the president of the Delaware Valley ICCA chapter from 1998 to 2002, and is currently serving a third term on the ICCA National Board of Directors. She is a frequent speaker at Advent software user group meetings and at such conferences as Schwab, Lightport, FiServ and Ashland. She is the author of numerous articles on custom reporting and programming hints and tips.

So... you're the greatest programmer ever. Your code is pristine, your documentation cogent and coherent. You communicate well with users and managers... and now you want to parlay these skills into a business. You want to transform yourself from a programmer into a consultant, and you want to be in demand. You want to set yourself apart from the field. You want customers to call you, to seek you out, to ask for you by name.

If this sounds like you, read on. This chapter is written with you in mind. The key to becoming a recognized name is getting your name out there. Write articles, write newsletters, speak at conferences, speak at user groups. What follows is a roadmap. It is meant to be a guide to get you on the road to recognition.

Find Your Niche

The first step on the path to becoming a recognized expert is to find your niche. You might be the world's greatest .Net programmer or SQL Server admin. Instead of focusing on the technology, however, determine the business or industry in which you have substantive knowledge.

A decade ago, my company had a technology focus. We were experts in "screen scraping" (yes, I know I'm dating myself here), having mastered several vendor packages and the Microsoft Visual Basic® expertise required to support them. Having the foresight (okay, the blind luck) to see that the need for these skills might decline over time, I accepted a contract assignment as a project manager with a large mutual fund firm. This firm was launching a new service offering personal financial advice and guidance to high net worth individuals. They needed software to support this offering.

As a part of this assignment, I went with my customers to a vendor conference in San Francisco. I saw a ballroom full of 1,000 companies and decided to myself, "I can make a business out of this!" From that day forward, I decided that my company, CSSI, was going to focus on the financial services industry. Even more specifically, we focused on Portfolio Management Systems, or Portfolio Accounting Systems. This type of software is used by investment management firms to aggregate a client's holdings in order to provide a complete financial picture. Components of the software are used for Customer Relationship Management (CRM), for trading, for forecasting, for income projections… The list goes on and on.

Installing, customizing and enhancing these packages requires a great deal of investment industry knowledge. It helps to know how various investment instruments behave, and what "looks right" in terms of performance and returns. I decided this was going to be our niche because I had investment and banking expertise from years of past projects (and because of the ballroom full of 1,000 potential customers).

Take inventory of your past projects. Have you been involved with projects in a specific industry? Perhaps you've learned the ins-and-outs of a specific vendor's software.

Learn the Language

Once you have decided to focus on a specific business or industry, learn the language of the business or industry. Many industries share programming languages, but each industry has its own lingo. Refer to Jason Harrison's chapter on "Business Speak" for examples that highlight how learning the business language sets you apart from other programmers and consultants.

For example, the investment industry contains terms such as reinvested dividends, short sells, boxed positions, withholding, multicurrency, forward swaps, hedge funds, private equity, GIPS, and, of course, audits and SEC. Every niche has a glossary of terms completely dedicated to the industry. Health care, insurance, manufacturing, distribution, banking, construction, retail, grocery... No matter what the business, you will find a veritable alphabet soup of terms, and a vocabulary that make sense only to those "in the know." You want to learn the language of your industry.

To learn the language, you'll need to get an education. Read, read, read! If you're on a project, let the managers know that you want to learn more about the industry, and ask for a recommended reading list. Are there certain books that are a "must read?" In the financial industry, "must read" books would include "After the Trade is Made"[4] by David Weiss, "The Handbook of Fixed Income Securities"[5] by Frank Fabozzi, "How the US Securities Industry Works"[6] by Hal McIntyre, and many others.

Stay current in your chosen niche by figuring out which newsletters, periodicals, and magazines are widely read by middle and top-level management. What are the decision makers reading? When you walk by their cubicles, what magazines are lying around? What periodicals are stacked up in the lunch room?

In my case, I learned about investment industry magazines completely by accident. Remember the conference with the ballroom full of 1,000 potential customers? When I returned from the conference, I found to my surprise that I was now on a mailing list for at least a dozen magazines. I was inundated with industry periodicals! Instead of reacting negatively to the sudden additions to my mailbox, I found myself delighted by the opportunity for education.

---

[4] Weiss, David. "After the Trade Is Made: Processing Securities Transactions." Third Revised Edition. Portfolio Cover, August 17, 2006.

[5] Fabozzi, Frank. "The Handbook of Fixed Income Securities." Seventh Edition. McGraw, 2006.

[6] McIntyre, Hal. "How the US Securities Industry Works." Third Edition. The Summit Group Publishing, Inc., October 1, 2007.

Describe Yourself in Terms of Your Niche

You've found your niche. You've read the "must read" books, and you're continuing your education by reading industry magazines and newsletters. By now, you've taught yourself to speak the language. You know what problems managers are facing. You are aware of impending legislation and subsequent impact to systems, people and processes.

Now it's time for you to learn to describe your skills and services in these industry terms. What specific business problems have you solved? How have you helped your customers? Don't just say you help them save time, money, reduce errors, increase efficiency. Be descriptive. For example, you didn't "develop a utility to allocate cash among accounts." Rather, you "developed a tool to automate cash allocations so that investment managers could comply with Carve Out requirements newly adopted in the 2010 GIPS standards."

Publish for Your Niche

Once you understand business challenges, start writing about them. You have something to say, and you know how to say it using language that managers will understand. Write about a specific method to solve a business problem. Write about several ways to solve a business problem, and discuss the pros and cons of each.

One of the most valuable lessons I ever learned was at an ICCA conference in San Jose, CA in 1999. One of the speakers suggested that the best way to build a business and a reputation is to give away some part of your skill set for free. I took that advice to heart, and it has turned out to be one of the best things I've ever done. When I started writing, I found it easier to educate my customers. I enjoyed teaching them techniques and methods to solve some of their problems. My goal was to teach them enough to solve the small problems on their own, and hope they would engage me to help solve the larger problems.

Launch your writing efforts with a series of "How To" articles. Teach your customers something. Demonstrate that you understand the industry and that you have solved problems in the industry.

Remember all that reading I told you to do a few paragraphs ago? The industry magazines, newsletters, and periodicals? This is the ready-made market for your educational articles. Not only were you reading to learn the language and needs of your niche industry, you were compiling information on potential publishing outlets. Associations, software vendors, certifying bodies, and user groups all have newsletters and websites.

A long time friend and fellow ICCA member, Gloria Metrick, focuses her business, GeoMetrick Enterprises (***www.geometrick.com***). on Laboratory Information Management Systems. She writes for industry journals and periodicals. She also publishes an electronic newsletter, *Out on a LIMS*. When asked how writing helped her build her business, she replied:

> Writing helps me in different ways, depending on where I write. I write in my industry's magazines to create credibility, and writing for peer-reviewed journals gives an even greater amount of credibility, although it is extremely time-intensive to write for these journals. I don't find it good for business as much as for bragging rights. There are certain periodicals that are also good for driving leads as they have the right mix of readers to do so. I write for my newsletter more to help stay in contact with people and remind them of what I do.
>
> I have also received business from writing responses both in my industry's discussion lists and in social networking sites. Even though I participate in these areas more to gain and share information, they are also good places to create name recognition for oneself.

I find that professional groups and user groups welcome articles that are educational in nature. As long as your article focuses on teaching the customer, as opposed to marketing to the customer, you will have a willing and receptive publisher. Be sure you include a description of your services (in business terms) in the "About the Author" section of your article. Include a link back to your website and make sure your article is on your website.

Due to space limitations, most newsletter publishers will limit the size of your article. Condense your article to fit into the space permitted by the publisher. Tell your readers that they can get the full article on your website.

Here's another golden nugget of business-building knowledge for you. (I learned this golden nugget at the ICCA Conference in Denver in 2002.) When your readers come to your website to download the full version of your article, let them gain access to your knowledge base of articles, but only after they've given you their name and email address. This is your opportunity to gather information on prospective customers.

If you are having trouble finding user group newsletters or other printed publications for your articles, consider "self-publishing." In today's environment, it's relatively easy to get "into print" by writing a blog, writing for someone else's blogs, or writing articles for your own website. Use social networking sites such as LinkedIn, Facebook, and Twitter (or whatever is currently most popular among your audience) to get the word out and direct your targeted audience to your website.

Write how-to articles, giving away some part of your knowledge. User groups, vendors, associations, and certifying organizations will all be willing to publish educational material. Use that educational material to draw people to your website, where you have even more educational material to give them. Firms are more than willing to give you their name and email address in exchange for access to your treasure trove of How To articles. Make sure you have plenty of marketing material available, too!

Become a Public Speaker

By this time, you're highly educated, well written, and widely published. You have a website that draws customers to your doorstep. You have more projects coming in than you know what to do with. You've hired employees or subcontractors to handle the overflow of work. Naturally, your next step is to become even busier by taking on speaking engagements.

You've developed relationships with the user groups, associations, certifying organizations, and vendors. Are there any regular meetings within driving distance? Most meetings will have a speaker or two. Tell the meeting organizer that you'd like to speak at one of the meetings, and send an email describing your topic. As with your articles, keep the talk educational and informational. Unless you are a vendor who is sponsoring the meeting, you should not use the opportunity to market your services. You are there to teach, to educate, to inform. Of course, have your marketing material ready, and include it with the handouts of your presentation.

Gloria describes the importance of educating clients and customers.

> If you try to include valuable information to help people out, and if people understand you genuinely want to help them with your information, they will sometimes feel not just that you are an expert in your field, but will also have good feelings about the type of person that you are. Over time, that good will can cause people to remember you and to feel that they *should* refer you, not that they have to, not that you asked them to, but that you *deserve* it. Getting business that way not only makes you feel good, and is good for your business, but I find these types of customers to be usually excited to work with you and often a great pleasure for you to work with, too.

If you don't mind traveling, try to arrange customer visits in and around the association meetings. Show your willingness to pay for your own travel if you have the means. You are building your reputation as a capable, willing educator. You're always ready with some unique training tip, some small tweak which solves an annoying problem. Once you get the reputation of being an educator, you will discover that invitations will come to you. You will no longer have to seek out speaking engagements. Event organizers will find you.

Unbeknownst to her, speaker and author Naomi Karten has been my guide for many years. She speaks on such subjects as Service Level Agreements, Customer Expectations, and Presentation Skills. I heard her speak at an ICCA meeting in Philadelphia several years ago. I subscribed to her newsletter shortly thereafter, and have been following and learning from her (online) ever since. See her website, ***www.nkarten.com***, for past issues of *Perceptions and Realities*, her entertaining, engaging, and educational newsletter.

She describes how speaking and writing create familiarity:

> Until the Web came along, speaking and writing were my primary means of creating name recognition—and they were (and still are) very effective. Back in the early days, it was via articles I submitted to print publications and featured columns I wrote for IT publications (though of course it wasn't known as IT back then). At one point, I wrote a bi-monthly column for a monthly magazine and people often told me they read my column every month. That helped me realize that once your name becomes familiar to people, they believe they are seeing it more often than they actually do. That meant that I didn't need to publish articles frequently, I just needed to do it regularly and consistently.

> The same thing happened with conference presentations. When I was scheduled to give more than one presentation at the conference, people told me, "Every time I turn the page [of the printed brochure], there you were." Which, of course, wasn't the case—my name and session appeared only 2 or 3 times. But I came to see the name recognition and credibility-building value of speaking at conferences. In fact, the publicity from the brochures were/are as valuable as the actual presentation in generating business. I often get calls from people who couldn't attend the event but saw my name listed and wanted help with the topic I was speaking on.

> As a result of all this speaking and writing, when I show up at speaking engagements, a lot of people already "know" me even though we've never met.

Support the Groups that Support You

I should add here that it never hurts to support the organizations and associations. Offer to sponsor an occasional breakfast or lunch meeting. Be open to supporting the organizations that promote your articles and those who extend offers of speaking engagements. If an organization is promoting your business by giving you an audience, then you want that association to remain vital and viable. Consider placing an advertisement in their newsletter, or becoming a meeting sponsor at some level.

You have proven that you can solve industry problems. You have demonstrated your willingness to write about those solutions. You have shown that you can speak eloquently and engagingly while educating and informing the audience. You keep a calendar of major industry events and conferences. You know which associations go to what conferences. You know where the user groups meet.

How do you get an invitation to speak at one of the major industry events? One way to become a speaker at conferences is to find out their proposal submission process, generally available on the conference website. Submit a proposal outlining your topic.

A second (and perhaps easier) way to secure a speaking invitation is to use the connections and relationships you've been nurturing. Most major industry conferences will have a user group track, or one or two sessions dedicated to an association of some kind. Ask the user group or the association if you can speak at their session. As you have done before, email the association organizer and describe your intended topic. In accordance with your reputation, be sure you keep the talk educational.

After Speaking, Look and Listen

Use your time at the conferences to visit all the booths in the exhibit hall. Get to know the vendors. Find out which other conferences they attend. Think of all of these vendors and exhibitors as extended family. You will find that you see each other at association meetings and at user group meetings. You go to the same conferences. They will become familiar with you and will have heard you speak at other events. When they have their major industry conference, ask for a speaking slot.

You will find that one opportunity leads to another, often unexpected, business relationship. Naomi Karten describes it this way.

> Although I'm a professional speaker and am paid by companies for my presentations and seminars, I've always believed in the importance of speaking at professional association meetings at minimal or no charge. I

believe that in every audience is someone who knows someone who knows someone who may someday want to hire me to speak, train or consult.

Gloria provides a concrete anecdote:

> Like other Marketing, writing and speaking can be used for cross-promotional purposes. On top of that, you can never tell what cascade of events it will cause. For example, I gave a talk to a small group of people merely to help out their organization. I enjoyed helping them and talking about what I do but had no expectations that I would get business from this particular mix of people. I probably never will get business from any of them. But one of them was at a conference, was listening to someone bemoaning the fact that they needed help, and she immediately thought of me and told him he should call me. Guess what?!?! He did just that and it turned into him becoming a client.

Naomi's books and handbooks have led to consulting and speaking engagements, even when the client never read the book/handbook:

> ...And books, of course, have been valuable in creating name recognition and generating speaking and consulting opportunities internationally. I've now published six books and am working on my seventh ("**Presentation Skills for Technical Professionals**"). In addition, my handbook on "**Establishing Service Level Agreements**" has been used by organizations worldwide (including places I never even heard of) for more than a decade. This handbook, plus my articles on SLAs, have led me to be seen internationally as an authority on this topic. Interestingly, many organizations have hired me to consult to them based on the existence of this handbook, without even seeing it.

Different Approaches

Let me close this chapter by mentioning that I outline the approach as writing, and then speaking. That is, the roadmap in the previous sections has you developing a reputation by writing articles and newsletters, and then using that reputation to secure speaking engagements. I do not mean to imply that this is the only approach to become a speaker and writer. I mean to say that this is the technique which worked for me.

Many speakers and writers, Naomi Karten among them, view writing and speaking as parallel efforts—things to be pursued at the same time, each independent of the other. Both Gloria and Naomi indicated that one effort leads to success in the other endeavor. Writings lead to invitations to speak, and speaking leads to requests to write books and articles. Either can lead to unexpected opportunities.

Remember that conference with the ballroom full of 1,000 customers? Three years later, I spoke at that conference, with that ballroom full of potential customers as my audience. I've spoken at many other industry conferences since then.

I'll never forget the Investment Management conference in Las Vegas, held at same venue as the Professional Bull Riding Association's championship event. I entered the maze of convention center hallways, made a right when I should have made a left, and ended up in the wrong exhibit hall. My goodness! Hanging from the ceiling were the enormous full color, full body photographs: 20-foot banners detailing the vital statistics of each of the athletes. Each banner was dedicated to a specific star. Fine male specimens, each and every one. Muscles, sinews, horns. I'm talking about the bulls, of course!

Wait, I digress. That's another story for another time.

Ethics and the Consulting Profession

Thomas "Tom" Warfield

Tom earned a Bachelor's degree from Capital University, and a Master's degree in Computer Science from George Washington University. For 12 years he worked at Claritas, the World Leader in Demographics, starting as a COBOL programmer and finishing as Manager of Data Warehousing. In 2000 he founded Warfield Consulting, specializing in Data Warehousing, Metadata, Data Conversion, and back-end web database support.

Tom holds certifications in Oracle and Microsoft, and has attended data warehousing classes at Ralph Kimball University. He has been a speaker at conferences held by the International Oracle User's Group (IOUG-A), and serves as the Secretary of the ICCA Greater Washington chapter. Tom splits his time between southern New Jersey and Arlington, Virginia. In his spare time Tom enjoys skiing, tennis, and running.

"Ethics is a maze of fuzzy lines and gray areas."

"Ethics is simple: There are rules, everyone knows them, and you either follow them or you don't."

Can both of these statements be true?

When I was studying Artificial Intelligence in graduate school, one of my professors gave a lecture about the "Scruffies" and the "Neats". The "Neats" believe everything happens according to rules. Every system has rules and must operate according to those rules, regardless of whether they are fully understood. The "Scruffies" believe there is room for ambiguity, non-determinism, and incalculability. They would argue that many problems are better solved by using some element of randomness.

"Neats" use expert systems and neural networks; "Scruffies" use Monte Carlo simulations and approximations. This is similar to the debate over predestination and free will. The point of the lecture was that both approaches have a place in Computer Science.

We are called upon every day to make hundreds of decisions, both large and small, both considered and subconscious. A person's sense of ethics is their strategy to make morally justifiable decisions. Everyone has such a strategy, even if they sometimes ignore it.

Earlier in my college days I took a course in Ethics. On several occasions, the professor would ask the class a series of questions. He would start with some lopsided moral dilemma where the "correct" answer was obvious. But then he would change the question, breaking it down or altering the conditions, so that the question got murkier and murkier. The professor would not give answers, he would just keep asking questions.

Finding the right answer was not the purpose of the exercise. Instead, it was to delve into that gray area, to isolate or narrow down the fuzzy line, and force the students to think. The result is what some people might criticize as "situational ethics" or "moral relativism". But it was clear that a slight change in problem conditions could change a student's decision about the right course of action.

That is the "Scruffy" position. On the other hand, the "Neats" can point to clear ethical rules that we all strive to uphold: avoid or disclose conflicts of interest, don't accept kickbacks, be honest.

Types of Ethical Lapses

An ethical lapse usually involves dishonesty, but not always. Most people try to behave ethically most of the time, or at least believe they do. But among the following three categories of ethical failures, only the first requires a conscious intent to misbehave:

1. Intentional: Stealing, lying, purposefully harming someone

2. Self-deception, including wishful thinking and rationalization

3. Genuine ignorance

Intentional Lapse

The first category doesn't require much discussion. The person knows they have done something wrong. They have willfully violated their own moral strategy.

Self-Deception

Self-deception is much more interesting. Suppose you are working for the government, where there is a rule that no vendor gifts exceeding $25 in value may be accepted. You are presented with a nice pen and pencil set, and the vendor left the original price tag on the bottom of the box: $35 MSRP. You could easily tell yourself, "Certainly my vendor, who is a clever fellow, would not have paid full price. He probably got it free, or bought it for 40% off at a discount store... Let's see, 40% off of $35? That's only... uh... $21! I'll take it!"

What has happened? The evidence is staring you in the face that you just broke the rules, although in a small way. Yet you fabricated a story that gives you moral justification for deciding to keep the gift.

The preceding example brings up another question: Does the degree of a violation make it more, or less, tolerable? Clearly if it was a thirty-five thousand dollar gold watch, it would be a different story and you would politely decline. A price tag of $3,500, $350, or even $99 might be high enough to make you turn down the gift. But what about $50? $45? Now the question becomes a fuzzy line—where is the cutoff? Do you figure out the exact price, $41.66, so that if you take %40 off, it would come out just under $25?

The "Neat" answer, of course, would be never to accept anything priced even a penny over $25. To the "Neat", the line has already been drawn, and it's not fuzzy at all: $25.01 would be just as unacceptable as thirty-five thousand.

By temperament, most computer consultants are more "Neat" than "Scruffy". This is because we study programming and think in terms of algorithms. In programming, we learn to use "truth tables" to fully evaluate all the possibilities. An algorithm is a step-by-step procedure that follows rules and logic, and leads to a definite result.

But a successful computer consultant must also be a business person to negotiate, sell oneself, and make deals. Even if it is contrary to our nature as computer experts, we have to be a little "Scruffy".

Ignorance

Ignorance can also lead to an ethical lapse. Suppose you were never told about the $25 gift limit, and you accept the $35 pen-and-pencil set without even thinking about it. Have you committed an ethics violation?

The answer is yes. Ignorance of the law is no excuse. It is your responsibility to be aware of ethical rules that have been established for your profession or workplace.

For example, if you are working in an office and charging by the hour, is it acceptable to eat lunch while working at your desk? Should you clock out while using the restroom or taking a coffee break? What about a smoke break? Is it okay to answer a personal phone call while on the clock? Or place a quick call to confirm a doctor's appointment? What about a phone call with a different client?

Expectations vary.

It is a good idea to have a policy regarding activities that are not part of the engagement, and review it with your client. In particular, if you are supporting many clients, each one should be aware that you might occasionally have to take calls from the others. If they are not unreasonably long, you don't bill one client for time spent on the phone with another, and you advise each client that this is your policy, most people will understand that it is a necessary part of your work.

But you should discuss your policy with each new client. It should never come as a surprise to one client if you are on the phone with a different client. If one of your clients thinks such calls are unacceptable, you should know that before the engagement begins. At that point you can decide whether to postpone phone calls while working for that client or turn down the engagement.

If a client insists that you must follow their policy, you must find out, and then follow, the guidelines they have established. You can ask to see the employee handbook, or at least the section pertaining to workplace behavior. It is not enough to just watch what your client's full-time employees do. They might not have read the handbook!

Here is another example of how genuine ignorance can lead to an ethical problem. At one point, when business was slow, I was trying to get some additional work. I decided to offer a generous bonus for anyone who would recommend me, if that recommendation led to a paying engagement. This was a terrific idea, I thought. Everybody wins! I get some new business, the new client gets the benefit of my skills and experience, and my buddy gets a nice slice of my gain.

Shortly after sending out emails announcing my new referral bonus program, I got a call from a former colleague. He said he would be happy to recommend me as someone who he knew would do an excellent job. But he would never accept a referral bonus for such a recommendation.

What's more, he would never agree to hire anyone based on someone's recommendation if he knew that it was "tainted" by a referral bonus.

I was startled, at first, by my colleague's reaction. But after reflection, my surprise turned to disappointment with myself. Of course he was right. What I was offering was effectively a kickback, practically a bribe. I had always thought of myself as a highly ethical person. How could I have done something like this? I learned that it is important to think, and think deeply, when making business decisions.

Ethics and People Around You

What should you do when you observe misconduct, even though you are not a participant? For example, what if you become aware that your client is using unlicensed software or submitting fraudulent documents?

We have all heard stories about whistleblowers and how they usually end up worse off personally than they would have been if they had kept quiet. To be a whistleblower takes courage, and might involve both personal and family sacrifice.

It is best to first work within the system, with internal grievance procedures, a company ombudsman, or senior management. But all too often, corporate behavior starts at the top, and these efforts may run into a dead end. At that point, if you have the stomach for it, it's time to get in touch with law enforcement or the media.

It might seem like some other professions have ethical standards that are more closely regulated than the consulting business. Consider lawyers, doctors, real estate agents, and CPAs. They are all subject to licensing, and they all have officially sanctioned grievance processes that can lead to license revocation.

Like journalists and politicians, at present, computer consultants aren't required to be licensed. We rely solely on public opinion and reputation. In a way, this makes ethical considerations even more important for us than for licensed professions. While you might trust a CPA just because he or she is a CPA, there is no implicit assurance that a consultant is honest and trustworthy just because he or she is a consultant. On the contrary, people are frequently suspicious of consultants, especially those who have not been in business for a long time.

Why is it important for the public to have confidence in professional integrity? Consider what happens when there is no such assurance. In many places in the world, ethical standards are loose or lacking among professions and society in general. Without ethics, there is corruption, fraud, bribery, conflict of interest, favoritism. Where corruption is tolerated, it eventually spreads throughout society and government. The result is like the Wild West, where life is unfair and everyone looks out for themselves. We need ethics for the same reason that we need laws. They are part of what makes us civilized. Ignoring ethics can destroy a career, a profession, even a country.

Ways to Show You Are Ethical

A good written moral guideline is helpful, but it is no substitute for having an internal moral compass and trustworthy friends. We must always be alert to ethical implications of what we say or don't say, of the business and financial decisions that we make every day, and of our own behavior. When there is a clear ethical line, stay on the right side of it. When there is a gray area that you can't avoid, seek advice, think it through thoroughly, and trust your own moral instincts. Even if you sometimes come up short, you will at least know that you always strive for the best.

The ultimate proof of your ethics is how you handle yourself, day to day and in ethically difficult circumstances. Until a client sees you do that (at work or elsewhere), all the client knows about your moral fiber is what you say and perhaps who you have chosen as associates. But if you publicly declare your adherence to an ethical code larger than your firm, and the code comes from a reputable source, that is strong reassurance for new clients.

This is one reason why the ICCA is vital to our success. All members pledge to honor ICCA's thorough Code of Ethics, which is included near the end of this book. As a member, I am fortunate to be able to include the Code as part of my business philosophy. It provides guidance in sticky situations. It also announces publicly that there is no point in asking me to do anything dishonorable.

As computer consultants, we work with some of the most sensitive aspects of our clients' businesses. In our field, integrity is anything but optional.

Soft Skills for Hard Situations

Jon Seidel, MBA, CMC

As the founder and President of EDP Consulting Inc., a consulting firm with clients nationwide, Jon has had an evolving and dynamic career— from his earliest education and experience as an engineer and high-tech specialist to his current focus on connecting business and technology. Jon is a leading expert on getting the most out of people as the single most important ingredient in any successful enterprise. With that theme in mind, he has established himself as an expert in business, organizational, and technology turnarounds.

With an incisive approach, Jon—alone or with one of his teams—works with a company or division, gains intimate knowledge of the immediate IT problem as it relates to the business, and specifies immediate and long-term solutions. He is relentless in his willingness to tell the truth at the highest levels of the organization, and he is listened to with remarkable attention because his results are evident in real dollars.

Jon's areas of focus are organizational and technology turnaround specialist, coach/mentor, and expert legal witness. Whether serving as a shadow CIO, consultant to the highest levels of management, software development expert, giving a speech or seminar, or testifying as an expert witness, Jon's integrity, insight, and intelligence make him a standout problem solver.

As a computer consultant, you might think all you need to do is hone your technical skills and you'll be able to just work on your assigned tasks. Not so! You'll find that situations arise in your consulting engagements where you need to focus largely on other factors that have nothing to do with technology.

To be a successful computer consultant, you must be able to recognize and deal with critical issues that are outside of the technology arena. In my career as a consultant, I've seen and lived through a number of these situations. I've grouped these into 5 categories—which I call the 5 Ps—to help me recognize and deal with them.

1.   People—Regardless of the technology, people are involved. They may be users of the technology, or part of the development effort, or even doing the maintenance work. It goes without saying that people are "soft," not hard technology.

2.   Process—Whatever system you are working on, whether it's a personal computer, a network, or a software application, it must operate within the business environment that uses it. That involves some kind of business process that incorporates the technical system. It may be as simple as the process for reporting errors when something crashes, or it may be a core business process (such as taking an order, paying a bill, or generating an invoice) that uses the technology that you are implementing.

3.   Planning—On the surface, you may think that planning is straightforward: just haul out Microsoft Project® or Artemis Schedule Publisher®, enter your tasks, and away you go. But consider that every organization approaches planning differently. Tasks have to be done by people and that is not a technology issue.

4.   Politics—This is potentially the bane of any consultant. You may think that as a consultant, you are immune to company politics. Sorry, but that's not the case. In fact, you may even find yourself a target of political actions.

5.   Public Relations—Communication and education (the essence of PR) are critical to success in any technology engagement. You may do a bang-up job of solving the technical problem; but if the user doesn't understand it, or if they don't know what you're doing and what you have done, they won't be happy and you won't be successful.

By way of example, I'll give you a personal case study for each of the 5 Ps so you can see how this plays out in the real world.

People

Case Study

I was engaged as a project manager for a large financial services firm to help them select a package for their data retention function. In this case, I was engaged through a broker, which turned out to be a key factor.

The "technical" side of this engagement revolved around learning their requirements, interviewing various vendors, visiting customer sites, and documenting the results. I worked directly with the manager of the data retention department and the associated IT manager. First I described the overall Scope of Work, which defined the deliverables expected, and then kept them in the loop as to my progress.

The work went quickly and relatively effortlessly, as the team was good to work with and the assignment was straightforward.

When I finished my report and submitted it upon completion of the assignment, I also submitted my final invoice. Much to my amazement, I received word back from the broker in a few days that my work was "unacceptable" and they were not going to pay my invoice. The broker's comment was, "Well, they're unhappy so we're going to write it off and therefore we won't pay you!"

As you might imagine, that was unacceptable to me. I called the IT manager with whom I had worked (and who had given me a written letter of reference as well). She told me that after the team reviewed my final report, the Senior Vice President in charge of the department took a look at the report and said: "This is not what I wanted at all. I expected [a lot more]..." The VP said she wouldn't pay the invoice. The IT manager attempted to reason with the VP but got nowhere, in spite of the fact that I had an approved Scope of Work and had met it fully.

I explained this to the broker who, while claiming to understand the situation, refused to try to collect the invoice. The broker claimed, "I know you did what you were asked to do, but they're a big client of ours and we don't want to upset them, so we still won't pay your invoice."

The only resolution available for this situation was to tell the broker that if they did not pay, I would go back to the client and work my way up the chain of command until I got to someone who would listen to reason and pay the several thousand dollars that were owed to me. Given that position, the broker relented and paid my invoice, in spite of the fact that they never did get the money from their client.

Learning

This case brought home the fact that people can be irrational and sometimes they can have an impact on your business—even if they are not actively involved with the project.

I also learned the importance of putting engagement terms—in detail—into a written Scope of Work before you start on the engagement. If I had not had this document, it would have been a simple "He said, she said..." situation and in that case, the consultant always loses.

Other People Situations

I've also had cases where

- people didn't want to do work that was assigned to them, or

- people bent the truth to avoid having to do work or avoid admitting to problems, or

- people covered up incompetence.

In all these cases, the people—their characters and personal attributes—were a significant factor and could make or break the success of the engagement.

Process

Case Study

I was asked by a consultant colleague to take over a small software development effort that his firm had started but would be unable to finish. My colleague anticipated that this would require little effort because the system had a development package to automate much of the effort in creating screens and connecting them to indexed sequential files where the data would reside. He had started development and then turned it over to me.

As I began work on the engagement, it rapidly became apparent to me that the processes involved were not understood—processes by which jobs were opened, information collected, labor posted to the jobs, materials ordered, supplies paid for and posted to the jobs, or bills calculated and produced. Even more discouraging, there were two operating divisions that did different work but used the same approach to billing... almost. The administrative division had to deal with constant inconsistencies in the billing process which slowed things down and resulted in billing delays.

Trying to accommodate all the differences between the two operating divisions would have significantly increased the cost and delivery time of the system. In addition, the manager of one division was unresponsive. I was heading for a disaster unless we clarified and agreed upon what the current process was and how it would change when the new system was implemented.

Fortunately, the Director understood these issues when I explained them, and authorized a new engagement to work through the process before continuing with software development. This phase began by getting key players from each department into a room and documenting the existing process flow through a facilitated session.

I used Warnier diagrams[7] (also called Warnier/Orr diagrams) to help me facilitate because they were easy to explain. As the review session progressed, the employees were able to understand what was being developed and comment on it. I also liked these diagrams because they were easy to draw and modify freehand and were visually very effective in outlining the process and highlighting issues.

During the process review, we focused *solely* on what they were currently doing with their paper and manual procedures. At this point we did not mention what the computer might or might not do for them. I've found over the years that once I introduce computers into the mix, people can get sidetracked and focus on "gee-whiz" technology, losing sight of the fact that basic business processes are key to bringing all the pieces together into a coherent whole. After we understood the current process, we were in a position to make informed decisions as to how the new process should operate. This was an early case of business process re-engineering... before the term had even been invented.

Besides learning what I needed to know to continue developing the computer system, the Director learned that the two divisions did almost the same work, with some discrete (now identifiable) differences. Essentially, there were two groups doing the same thing, albeit with somewhat different procedures and paperwork. This knowledge allowed the Director to combine administrative components of the two divisions into one unit. This was done over time, allowing for normal job transitions, and achieved a 25% reduction in administrative expense—and this was done without creating a single computer program.

We subsequently implemented the system very successfully and maintained and expanded it over a period of many years. As we

---

[7]   See   ***http://varatek.com/warnierorr.html***   and
http://en.wikipedia.org/wiki/Warnier/Orr_diagram   for more information.

approached Y2K (the transition to year 2000), I recommended to the Senior Director that they scrap the system rather than attempting to upgrade it, so it was replaced. But it served the department for almost 19 years… all because we looked at the process first.

Learning

- Whenever it comes to computer systems, technology is only one piece of the system. Process is what ties the business and the technology together.

- Systems need to be approached with a fresh perspective. This is why it is often so valuable to have someone analyze a system *without* detailed knowledge of the industry or business. Naïve questions sometimes produce brilliant answers.

- As a side note, exercise care when taking over another person's work. You need the "right to review and modify," and that needs to be clear up front.

Other Process Situations

A frequent client complaint bemoans the fact that "everyone has their own way of doing things." This is wasteful and error-prone and makes it much harder to implement effective computer systems. Either you have to create multitudinous exceptions, or everyone complains that the system doesn't work right. Either case is a problem for you as the computer consultant, because either implementation cost increases or customer satisfaction decreases. In my experience, you ignore business processes at your peril.

Planning

Case Study

When it comes to planning, there is a tendency to assume that Microsoft Project® or Open WorkBench® (originally Project Workbench®, now open source) is all you need. Describe some tasks, identify who will do those tasks, get an estimate, and then just track the results and produce your charts and statistics. Even though that may be the impression one gets from looking at many of the details associated with planning, it isn't entirely true.

On one engagement, I was brought in to help a troubled project. An ERP implementation for a mid-sized computer manufacturer was severely late and over-budget, but completion of the project was critical. My first efforts to get started met significant resistance: no one wanted to commit to the project. For one thing, they had all decided it was going to be a failure and they didn't want to be involved with it.

Eventually, I got team leaders assigned to the project—four in all; one for each major user/business area being affected. As I started working with the team and developing a project plan, we persistently ran into difficulty getting the team leaders to understand what the tasks were and what they needed to deliver. One team leader in particular found it difficult to come up with definitions and deliverables. He needed every possible step in the process called out on the project plan. He functioned on what I call the "operational process" level as opposed to the "planning" level, and wanted more detail than I had assumed would be required.

After a couple of attempts to educate him in classic project management techniques, I switched gears, threw out the guidelines, and developed an approach that satisfied his need for understanding and also worked for the whole team. We literally drove our planning tasks down to the hour-by-hour level where necessary for our "operational level" team leader. We wound up with much smaller tasks than we would otherwise have blocked out. It didn't hurt the plan (aside from making it bigger) and it provided a comfort level he needed to move forward.

Although we didn't have a sign-off sheet for each of those small hour-by-hour tasks, we had significant rollup and milestone tasks that provided key deliverables for the overall project. This allowed us to use another planning component that is part of standard project management: sign-offs of each delivered component, at the rollup or milestone level.

We requested our first sign-off upon completion of the overall project plan. Team leaders took it to each of their Vice Presidents. After several days, at last we had sign-offs from each of the area VPs and we were ready to go.

The sign-offs? They were displayed on the outside of my cubicle as a constant and publicly visible reminder to everyone that the powers that be had approved this effort and gave us the go-ahead to proceed. These sign-offs proved to be a critical piece in continuation of the project.

Learning

- Planning is a people process. People identify the tasks, estimate the effort, produce the schedule, and then do the work. We have to take the individual needs and knowledge of people we work with into consideration and make adjustments accordingly.

- Planning is central to success on consulting engagements. It's an important communication tool (see PR below) and is a key element in achieving consensus for the road ahead.

- Even a simple planning tool like a "Scope of Work" (see the People section above) can have a major impact on our engagements.

- Planning, when done correctly, includes responsibility, accountability, and commitment by the parties involved. Without these elements, the project won't be truly successful.

- Getting sign-off on elements of the project means that decision-makers have to think about what they are signing and then take responsibility for their decisions. Making those sign-offs public lets everyone know where decision-makers stand.

Other Planning Situations

I have worked with clients where the planning process was essentially non-existent. As a result, they wandered off on tangents without making real progress. They wasted huge amounts of effort and money. I have also seen clients who spend too much time planning everything in minute detail with generally negative results—a hazard I had to avoid for the overall project in my example, even though one of my teams needed more detail than normal.

Politics

Case Study

As a computer consultant, you may believe politics don't matter to you: "I'm a consultant and I'm not a part of company politics." You may even have become a consultant because you wanted to get away from politics. (That was one of my beliefs when I started my consulting business in 1979.) As I learned, sometimes painfully, politics exist wherever you go and you can be targeted as a consultant just as easily as the client's employees (maybe even more so).

The client I mentioned in the Planning section was fraught with politics. The VP of Manufacturing publicly supported the project to convert from ManMan® to the new Enterprise Resource Planning (ERP) system, but privately did not want the project to succeed. As a result, work to be done in his department suffered from foot-dragging. I heard rumors of this, but had nothing concrete with which to verify them. (There can be other reasons for foot-dragging.) When I met with him, he was pleasant, conversational, and—on the surface—very open and helpful.

During the planning process that I described, he always had questions and concerns about what was to be accomplished and how it could be done. That was at least one reason why his team leader came back with more and more questions about tasks and deliverables. While it is true that the team leader was driving the detail so that he could be comfortable, it was also true that the VP was playing a delaying game.

Forcing the project plan to a micro-level eventually made everything so clear that the team leader was comfortable and took it to the VP for sign-off. I was told some time later that the VP was speechless when he saw the plan and took three days to review it with a fine-tooth comb. He was unable to find any flaws that he could legitimately reject and had to approve it—with his signature. Once that signed approval went up on my office, I knew we had a chance of success.

Following the planning effort, we realized that we needed one more month to complete the project. That was approved, and we commenced work. As we progressed, sign-offs accumulated on my wall. When the "Go-NoGo" decision point was reached just before implementing the system, I went around the table for the senior managers to give the thumbs up. The Manufacturing VP looked at me and said, "Well, I guess at this point I can't say 'no', can I?" He was obviously referring to the sign-offs which the project team had accumulated, with his signature on several key documents. My response was, "If you have critical issues, you're certainly free to say we're not ready." He said "Go" and we implemented the project, with all features operational.

That isn't the end of the story. About four weeks later, while working on Phase 2 of the overall implementation plan, the IT Director called me into his office. He closed the door and said, "I've been fired and they're going back to ManMan®!" The VP had shifted the fight to another venue, bringing in a big-name consultant firm to "audit" the system we had installed. Their recommendation said, "You never should have tried to go to this new system. Go back to the old one." Over the next several months, the client and the big-name consultants undid what we had done and reverted to ManMan®.

This was a company of roughly $80+MM revenues. They spent almost $1.9MM on the initial implementation, most of it before I came aboard, and expected to spend another $400,000 on deimplementation.

Learning

- Politics is _always_ a factor to a certain extent—it's just uglier in some cases.

- Never believe you can *win* at client politics—sometimes the most you can do is make sure you aren't slaughtered in the process.

- Don't get too invested in the projects you work on. In the final analysis, it's the client's money, their company and their decision.

Other Politics Situations

I've been in several situations where clients treated me kindly and kept smiling as they sidelined the project or group. I've seen situations where political favoritism resulted in lack of progress or outright obstructionism, and cases where many people in the company were afraid to act because of a political situation.

I've learned to take this into account when going into a new project and have instituted my own methods for interviewing people "on the ground" and learning what's going on. That saved my bacon more than once.

Public Relations

Case Situation

I was the acting IT Director for a leading database management company. Our group faced the unenviable task of changing the company's email policies. I worked with the company's chief counsel to resolve two issues:

- Our email servers were massively overloaded with mail that had been kept by the employees. Many of them saved old email messages as their personal memory. Some of the employees had been there for 8 years and had kept email throughout their entire tenure.

- The company had recently faced a series of lawsuits, leading to concern regarding the amount of information potentially accessible to a legal discovery process. As long as it was kept on the company's central servers, it was discoverable and who knew what off-hand comments might be contained there?

From a management perspective, we had to reduce the amount of data stored on various systems. The email system being used had actually exceeded its design limits, putting it at risk of a potentially catastrophic

failure. From a legal perspective, unrestrained email archival presented an open invitation for a legal field day.

From a technical perspective, this was quite easy:

- purge the old emails, leaving only 90 days worth of history

- clean up the email servers

- implement a regular purge to maintain a 90-day history

From a personnel perspective, it was a different story. We expected employees who had been around for a long time to be concerned about the impact this would have on their ability to access past emails and information. These were hard-core software engineers, who are not noted for mincing words when they're unhappy about something.

We sent an announcement to the employees, briefly explaining the situation and need for the change. In that email, we announced a series of "town hall" meetings to discuss the situation in more detail and answer any questions. (I've done such "town hall" meetings on several occasions. In fact, I met my wife at one many years ago—an unexpected benefit!) Prior to the public meetings, we also identified some of the key individuals in the company. I met privately with each them, so I could better understand issues that might be raised and see if they could understand our concerns.

The meetings were every bit as contentious as we anticipated. We were accused of destroying the "corporate memory," making it impossible for people to do their jobs, and worse. However, we treated these meetings as educational opportunities (after all, that's what PR is all about) and maintained a respectful position. "We're all working in the best interests of the company and—while difficult—there are good and valid reasons for what we are doing."

The turning point came when one of the senior engineering managers said to me:

> I don't like what you're doing, but at least you're talking to me and I understand your perspective.

In the end, we were able to implement the email purge, clean up the servers, and institute new rolling purge procedures. As a result, we saw an almost immediate improvement in email reliability and stability. Even though they missed their email history, the employees could see benefits of the program in this area.

Learning

This experience reinforced my strongly-held opinion that communication (and PR) can make or break a situation.

- Failure to let people know what's going on leads them to assume the worst.

- Failure to listen to people leads them to assume you do not consider them important.

- Either of the above conditions promotes anxiety, which is a recipe for disaster. The people whose support you need will make it a point to object to the process.

Other Public Relations Situations

Once upon a time, I was the Data Center Director for a large bank. The programming staff used IBM's TSO (Time Sharing Option, an early system allowing people to work from remote terminals). Unfortunately, TSO response was slow and although we were working to improve it, the programmers were dissatisfied. I held a town hall meeting in that situation with similar results: the programming staff weren't happy about the situation, but the fact that I talked with them and listened to their issues at least ensured that I would be given a chance to solve the problems.

Conclusion

If you get the technology right and the 5Ps wrong, it's pretty certain that the technology won't make any difference because it won't be accepted. If you get the 5Ps right, there still may be problems, but you'll be in a much better position to make your work succeed.

In the final analysis, we all want the work that we do to be used and have meaning—and soft skills are at the heart of making sure that happens.

Staying Marketable

Robert "Bob" McAdams

Bob began doing computer programming for money while he was in college. After college, he worked in the computer departments of insurance, engineering, and banking firms before becoming a software developer with Online Software International, Inc. in 1986. While he was at Online Software, Bob did major development work on a quality assurance and stress testing tool called Verify® and wrote about half of the IBM CICS® interface for a product called RAMIS®. When Online Software was bought out by Computer Associates International, Inc. in September of 1991, Bob started his own company, Fambright, where he has worked ever since.

Fambright became a member of the Independent Computer Consultants Association in 1992, and became one of the founding members of the Northern New Jersey chapter of the ICCA in 1994. Bob joined the board of directors of the Northern New Jersey chapter in 1996 and has, at one time or another, held every position on the board. He currently serves as chapter president.

Information technology is the most rapidly changing business I can imagine. The first Turing-complete electronic computers were built less than 75 years ago, which makes them newer than television, newer than the airplane, and newer than the liquid-fueled rocket. Those early machines were humongous contraptions that filled an entire room and cost a small fortune. Today we have computers that are vastly more powerful than those early models, but that fit in the palm of your hand and sell for a little over a hundred dollars.

To call this an enormous rate of change is an understatement! The computer business is a bit like medicine might be if the human body were evolving new organs every few years and radically changing its physiology every couple of decades.

Because of this, people who work with computers need to be constantly updating their skills. In large companies, every competently run IT department allocates money in its annual budget to train its employees in new technologies. But those of us who are computer consultants face a special problem: We are supposed to be experts, and clients don't usually perceive someone to be an expert in something just because they've attended a training class on it—they want someone who actually has experience working with it. Yet the way we get experience, as consultants, is by servicing contracts. In order for us to land the contracts, we need to be perceived as experts. To be perceived as experts, we first need to have experience.

For people who are new to the consulting profession this usually isn't a problem, because they already have marketable experience when they become consultants (whether we're talking about a 40-year-old who enters consulting after a couple of decades of employment with major corporations or a 21-year-old who enters consulting after doing web design as a teenager). Sooner or later, every consultant becomes aware that the industry has shifted, and expertise that once readily landed contracts has become, if not obsolete, at least nowhere near as marketable as it was before.

When that happens, we can get training in new technologies that are hot, but then we come face to face with a chicken-and-egg problem that, at first sight, might seem insurmountable: How can you land a contract where you can turn your training into experience when it seems that you need to already have experience in order to land the contract?

"Experience" Is a Package Deal

The key to solving this problem lies in recognizing that every contract invariably requires a number of different types of expertise. While a client might ideally like to have a consultant who has experience with every type of skill required for an assignment, this is often not a practical expectation. Most consulting assignments have some degree of urgency, so the client does not have an unlimited amount of time to find a consultant with an ideal skill set for the task. In such situations, the best fit for the assignment may be a consultant who is highly experienced with most of the skills required, but who has only had training (without experience) in one or two of those skills. The odds that this will be the case increase greatly when one or more of the following are true:

- The skills in which the consultant has training but no experience are perceived to be relatively minor parts of the assignment, as measured either by the percentage of the work that will involve the skill, or by the level of sophistication required, or both.

- The skills in question are so new that the number of consultants who have experience working with those skills is very limited.

- The client lacks the technical knowledge needed to evaluate whether the consultant has had experience working with the skills needed for the assignment, and must therefore rely on the consultant's personal assessment of his or her ability to complete the assignment successfully.

- The client feels that they know the consultant well enough to have confidence in his or her competence and integrity, and is therefore willing to rely on the consultant's assessment of his or her ability to complete the assignment successfully.

When you employ this approach, you are, in effect, using areas in which you are highly experienced as bargaining chips to buy your way into contracts where you can get experience using skills in which you only have training. Once you have gained experience using a new skill in a contract, it will become another bargaining chip that you can use in future contracts to gain experience with additional skills.

Use It Before You Lose It!

"Use it or lose it" is a familiar adage which describes the fact that we tend to lose things that we don't use. Muscles atrophy when we don't use them. Skills get rusty, in the figurative sense, if we don't keep practicing them. Equipment can get rusty, in the literal sense, when it's not used regularly.

But the reality in the computer consulting business is a bit harsher than this! Our skills eventually cease to be marketable even if we do use them. So the trick is to use our existing skills, while they are still highly marketable, to bargain our way into contracts where we can gain the new experience needed to keep us marketable.

This takes vigilance and planning. It takes vigilance because it is all too easy, when our businesses appear to be successful, to become content with contracts where we use only those skills in which we have already demonstrated proficiency and where it is therefore relatively easy to sell clients on the fact that we are experts. It takes planning, because we cannot afford to simply allow ourselves to drift into new skills without determining whether those skills are strategic in insuring our future marketability and success.

The single most important thing to remember is that, in the computer business, the clock is always ticking. It is only a matter of time before our current technical skills will lose their value, not only in providing us with an adequate flow of contracts, but also in providing us with opportunities to acquire experience with new skills.

Marketability Usually Depends on Technical Knowledge

An experienced consultant usually brings many things to the table besides knowledge of particular technologies. But a consultant's marketability is likely to depend to a substantial degree on having knowledge of the specific technologies and platforms a client uses or wants to use.

First, knowledge of relevant technologies will usually be much easier for a client to evaluate than the other types of expertise a consultant may have, such as problem solving ability, interpersonal skills, or the ability to manage a project and ensure that it is completed on schedule.

Second, in the computer business, technology is always relevant, even to non-technical aspects of a project. There are major differences between batch processing and an online environment, or between a system that runs on a network of terminals connected to a mainframe computer and a system that runs on the Internet. Design considerations are different. Testing and debugging considerations are different. Even if a client's real problem is non-technical in nature, there's a good chance that it may be impossible to fully understand it without knowledge of relevant technologies.

How can we develop a strategy for keeping our technical skills current?

Determining Where the Computer Industry Is Headed

Thirty years ago, IBM® was the dominant company in the computer industry. It had beaten its primary rival, Univac®, and became so large and so well entrenched that it appeared no one could ever dislodge it from its position of dominance. Then it made a serious mistake: It failed to anticipate how important personal computers were going to become.

It's easy to see why IBM® made this mistake. Conventional wisdom in those days was that mainframe computers were for big companies, minicomputers were for small companies, and personal computers were for individuals. IBM® reasoned that big companies have a lot of money, small companies have a little money, and individuals, by and large, have almost no money, so focusing on mainframes was the way to maximize profit. Reality today, of course, is that big companies have a lot of PCs, small companies have a few PCs, and individuals have one or two PCs. By failing to recognize and adapt early enough to the way the market was moving, IBM® lost its position of dominance.

If a company like IBM® could make a mistake like that, it's clear that figuring out where the computer industry is headed isn't easy. But if you *try* to figure out where it's headed, you're likely to come closer to the mark than if you don't try. Spend some time thinking about these questions:

- What aspects of the computer industry do you think will grow in the next 5 years, or 10 years, or 20 years? What aspects do you think will shrink? Why do you think these things will happen?

- Have you ever been wrong about where the industry was headed? If so, why did things go differently than you expected? Were you misinformed about some of the facts or did you analyze the facts incorrectly? Understanding your mistakes should help you make better predictions in the future.

- If you expect that usage of a particular technology is going to grow, do you expect the number of people providing services for that technology (either as consultants or as employees) to grow faster or slower than use of the technology? If you expect that use of a technology is going to shrink, do you expect the number of people providing services for that technology to shrink faster or slower than use of the technology? Keep in mind that the *ratio* of service providers to users is likely to determine how lucrative a technology will be for computer consultants.

- To what extent do you expect services for a particular technology to be provided by consultants rather than employees? Why?

Developing a Strategy

Once you have some idea of where the computer industry is headed, you can think about where you want to be in that industry. To some extent, this may be governed by what you've done in the past. (Keep in mind that it's usually easier to cross a stream than to cross an ocean.) To some extent, it will be determined by the kinds of things you like to do.

Next, begin to map out a strategy for how you can move in the direction you have chosen. Keep in mind that if your goal involves technologies far removed from those you worked with in the past, your existing experience may be of limited value in convincing clients that you are an expert in the technologies you want to work with now. You may need to make the transition in a series of smaller steps rather than all at once.

Remember that if you want to be an expert who can advise a client about which of several competing technologies to choose, there are few substitutes for getting hands-on experience with all of the competing technologies. You may be able to find reviews that compare the strengths and weaknesses of the different technologies, but the authors of those reviews, rather than you, will be the experts. One of your goals should be to gain enough breadth of experience to be in a position to write comparative reviews yourself.

It may be useful to visit some of the boards where computer consulting contract openings are posted. These postings are nearly always done by brokers. Even though you may not have any interest in working through brokers, the postings should give you some idea which technologies are currently in demand.

Especially look for contracts whose requirements you could nearly but not entirely satisfy. Make a list of technologies in which you would need to acquire expertise to satisfy the requirements for those contracts. Then analyze which of those technologies lie in the direction you want your consulting practice to move.

Those technologies are probably the ones in which you should take training, since they are the ones for which you are likely to be able to use your existing experience to get your foot in the door.

Keep in mind that "training" can mean anything from attending a class with a live instructor to getting books or manuals on the technology and studying them on your own. There are a wide variety of options for getting training in the computer field, so you should make your choice based on what works best for you.

In a few areas of the computer industry, well recognized and respected certifications are available. If your goal lies in one of these areas, it certainly makes sense to get the certification. But other areas have no established certifications, or the certifications available have poor standing to establish your reputation as an expert. Use your own judgment about whether certification is worthwhile.

After you acquire training in new technologies, actively look for contracts where you can gain experience actually working with those technologies for money. Keep the following in mind:

- Avoid assignments for which the client considers the new technology to be the core of the assignment. In such cases, their attention is likely to focus on the fact that you have merely been trained in that technology and have never actually worked with it. Instead, look for assignments where the focus will be on skills with which you have extensive experience.

- When talking with the client, place heavy emphasis on the fact that your experience in the technologies that constitute the core of the assignment is stronger than they are likely to find anywhere else, and your experience with those skills is critical to the success of the project.

- One of the most effective ways to convince a client that you are capable of handling an assignment is to present a clear, well thought out plan for how you intend to accomplish it. If you sound like you have a handle on what needs to be done, the client is likely to believe that you do.

- Once you have experience working with a particular technology, a client is likely to be swayed more by your knowledge of the technology (which may be a function of your training) than by the nature of your experience with it (which may be difficult for them to evaluate).

- One of the best tools for building your reputation can be success with a task on which others have failed. If you can solve a problem that a client's staff and/or another consultant failed to solve, or if you take over a project that is behind schedule and successfully bring it to completion, the client will have first hand evidence that you are a cut above your competition. But make sure that the client is actually looking for a successful resolution, rather than trying to find an outside vendor on whom they can dump the blame for a failure!

Try to keep track over time of how the experience you get in your contracts is (or isn't) helping you to advance toward your goal. The longer a contract lasts, the more important it is that it allows you to get experience with new technologies that will keep you marketable in the future!

Where to Find Information

Nancy A. Ridenhour, CDP, CCP

Nancy works with companies to analyze their current business technology, keeps them aware of technology changes and prepares them to handle those changes. This allows the companies to more correctly estimate costs and profits, manage time expenditures, prepare for customer impacts, and handle sudden changes easier.

Nancy received her Bachelor of Science degree in Statistics from North Carolina State University (NCSU) in 1976. She was employed in the textile and financial industries until 1990. She began consulting work in 1990 and formed her own business on January 1, 1993. Nancy worked on large projects in the banking and electric utility industry through 2003. In 2004 she decided to change the focus of the business to include small and mid-sized companies.

Nancy received her Certification in Data Processing in 1984. That same year she received her General Banking diploma from the American Institute of Banking. In 2003 she obtained certification as a woman-owned business from the Women's Business Enterprise National Council— Southeast. In 2007 Nancy received the Certified Computing Professional (CCP) designation. She has been a member of the Independent Computer Consultants Association since 1993. She is a member of the National Association of Women Business Owners. Nancy's activities for her alma mater include serving a term on the Alumni Board in the 1980's, three terms on the NCSU College of Physical and Mathematical Sciences (PAMS) Foundation Board and currently serving on the PAMS Alumni/Friends Advisory Board . Nancy also enjoys teaching a 5th grade Junior Achievement class each year and teaching a 6th grade Sunday school class once per month.

Just like the seasons change, so do our businesses and lives. We become aware of these changes through the information we receive. Our reception is dependent on the tools we use. These tools start with our eyes and ears and include cell phones and computers. Because information can be valid one day and out of date the next, top consultants use a combination of tools to obtain, validate and share information.

Be Observant

Use your senses to discover information. Most of us have two eyes, two ears, one mouth, two hands and two feet. We can see, smell, taste, talk, and travel. Most of us talk much more than we listen.

Practice listening more than speaking. When talking with people, I try to keep my mouth shut for most of the conversation, ask questions and listen. Most people love to talk and want to be helpful. Listening gives me information on many different areas. In one week I listened to a grocery store employee tell me about the process being used to quickly build some expensive houses near her home, and a business owner described the market she is serving. Both pieces provided me with interesting information to help with some plans I am making.

Take time to reflect on meetings, casual conversations, or things you happen to see and hear. A few years ago, I started taking time at least once per week to just sit and let my mind and body catch up. I am amazed at what my mind brings forward and remembers.

Notice signs, buildings and behavior patterns that you see each day. For example, while driving to a meeting recently, I noticed a number of "For Sale" and "For Rent" signs in an upscale neighborhood. That told me how deep the banking problem is in my region. I also noticed the businesses that are still open and the offices or storefronts that are empty. In my neighborhood, I recently noticed that more people are at home. Some are working from home, others are looking for work, and some have retired.

Keep track of what family and friends are doing. When was the last time you listened about what they are doing? When was the last time you let them know what you are doing? I learn what is going on in some companies just by talking with neighbors.

Be Involved

Volunteer in your community. This is a great way to meet people, learn about what is going on in the area, give back to the community, and let people get to know you.

Allow people to see how you work when you are not receiving cash compensation. It can be short term or long term. For example, I teach a Junior Achievement® course to a fifth grade class each year. It takes only five visits to the school. I get information about the school and the thoughts of the students.

Stay in touch with your alma mater. Colleges and universities now have alumni clubs throughout the United States and online social network groups.

If it has been a while since you contacted your alma mater, get back in touch. Let them know where you are and what you do. Volunteer to assist them. I present college scholarships at local high schools. The university sends me a basic speech and guidelines. I then make changes where needed for the time allotted and the situation.

Be Connected

Let people find you online. You need to have at least one website. I have heard of people with several, since they have different businesses. Just make sure your data is accurate. The truth will come out. Word spreads fast, and lingers, because of online communication tools. The damage from an online error may not ever be corrected.

Join at least one social networking site. Connect there with people you know. Also check the site's group listings. If you are a member of any, then add those to your connections. Request to join any of the site's groups that you are interested in and pertain to your business. Periodically note what you are doing.

Participate in discussion groups. Answer questions on social networks only if you have valuable information to share. The information will be appreciated and you will gradually become recognized as an expert in that area. Do not bluff or just answer to say you provided an answer. The "good citizen" rules apply today more than ever because of the global reach of social networks online.

Read, Write and Learn

Write a blog. You can maintain it as part of your website or use one of the free blog services to post your ideas.

Use a different blog for unique purposes. I participate in two. I use Blogger® to post my personal weekly one. I also write for the ICCA blog periodically. Each blog allows people to get to know me, which lets me start building a relationship with them.

Check the websites of major technology companies. Start with IBM®, Microsoft®, and Oracle®. This will lead you to others. On the websites, look for webinars and white papers that pertain to your business area. This also gives you information to share with other people.

Register to receive advanced notice of webinars. This allows you to listen and ask questions of the speaker if appropriate. I receive emails every day about upcoming webinars. I also receive emails that have links to white papers, and recordings of webinars which I can listen to online or download to an iPod®.

Attending webinars or registering for notices can also bring telephone calls from company representatives. I appreciate the opportunity to talk with them for a few minutes and I receive more information on their product.

Search for learning establishments in your area, including training facilities. Every year, many colleges and universities offer special classes. You do not have to get a degree. You can take a course that counts toward certification credits that you need. You will meet other professionals, and you will acquire information to share with others.

Be ready for special learning experiences. One of my favorites has been the Management Development Program that the Harvard Business School® (HBS) alumni group offers in my region. This is a fourteen week case study program. It shows another view of the business world.

Take advantage of "extras" offered by the learning opportunities. The HBS program also allowed me to join the local HBS alumni group and attend their meetings. They bring in CEOs and Harvard professors to speak. They also have joint meetings with other MBA alumni groups in the area. I do not get direct business from the group, but I learn about business trends.

Ask people about the media they read. Also research online for any regional, national, or international papers and magazines that have information on the people, businesses or groups that interest you. For any print publications that catch your attention, find out where you can get a copy and read it.

Try several different publications. See which ones you like. Then subscribe to the ones that give you helpful information. You can subscribe to online editions, print, or both. Print editions often have more detailed information than online editions of the same publication.

Be open to adjusting your subscriptions. I started by subscribing to one business newspaper, since I already subscribed to the regional paper. I now subscribe to three business papers in my region. They each cover the news in a different way. From one of them, I also obtain daily email updates, as well as daily updates from two of the sister publications in other parts of the state and updates from their national office. Sometimes information is provided by one of the sister publications or the national that I find useful and did not receive from the local one, or it may appear in a sister publication before it appears locally.

Join Business and Professional Groups

Do periodic searches for technology and business associations in your area. Check for the Service Corps of Retired Executives (SCORE®). See if your area has a group of these retired business executives to help businesses start up and grow. Check government sources such as the Small Business Administration (SBA) and see what they offer. Find out what the local Chamber of Commerce® provides. You will be amazed by how these groups and their offerings can change during a short time. Routinely visit their websites and some of the other websites where they are noted.

Search for associations that may not have a local chapter but may be important to your business. You will want to search on the industry that you are in and on industries of your clients.

Learn to be an active member across geographical boundaries. I joined the Independent Computer Consultants Association in 1993 when I formed my business. ICCA does not have a local chapter. However, I am always energized by the information that I learn from the newsletter, webinars, discussion groups, conferences and activities such as writing this book chapter.

Travel to conferences. I nearly always travel to the annual ICCA conferences, which are held in a different city each year. I meet people from many parts of the country and learn about business trends they are seeing. I have also met people whose product or service I needed. I take at least one day to tour the area and gain insights about the area businesses.

Look for groups where you may not wish to be a member, but can participate. Women Business Enterprise National Council (WBENC®) does not have a local group. Its members are major corporations. WBENC® certifies women-owned businesses. They have certified me as a woman business owner, and my state is included in the Georgia-based group. I receive event information from them that allows me to attend WBENC® meetings in North Carolina, South Carolina or Georgia. This allows me to network with major companies and other WBENC®-certified companies.

Be more than a member once you have joined a group. Join a committee. You will learn to know people better in the small group. Also, you will learn to know others in the larger group when you are doing things for the committee at meetings. They will also learn to know you.

Attend Local Events

Select local events to consider attending. Find the contact information. Learn more by sending an email or making a phone call. If you send email, in the Subject line, include the group and event name. Allow a couple of days to receive a response. The contact may be a volunteer juggling the event with their regular job.

If you register to attend but later find that you cannot, notify your contact as soon as possible. You would expect the same courtesy of people who sign up to attend your events.

Plan to arrive about ten minutes before the event begins and try to have time to linger after the meeting. You will be amazed by what you learn before and after meetings. I try to notice the non-verbal as well as the verbal. You may notice which people are normally late, always answering a cell phone, or do most of the talking and very little listening.

Ask for a business card if you meet someone whose contact information you want to keep. Look over the card when you receive it. Ask at least one question or make a comment about something on it. I make notes on the cards because notes are better than relying on my memory.

Within a week, enter the business card information into your system. If you promised something to the person, meet that delivery deadline. If the two of you said that you were going to meet, contact them within twenty four hours to schedule the meeting.

Stay Open to What's New

Constantly be open to new opportunities to receive and share information such as Twitter®. Revisit venues you are not currently using. Investigate them and have fun watching, listening, sharing, and reviewing information.

Remember—the tools you can use to find information change, but the principles stay the same.

Cornerstones of Successful Project Management

David A. Zimmer, PMP

David, whose American Eagle Group specializes in project management training and consulting, uses his 30 years of project management experience to mix theory with everyday reality, creating sound practices for his clients. One company shortened its manufacturing cycle by two weeks and lowered defect rates by 25% using the ideas he presented. He teaches industry-accepted project management standards based upon the Project Management Body of Knowledge (PMBOK®)[8] so students learn the proper processes, with tangible examples, enabling them to implement the newly gained knowledge at work the next day. Each seminar attendee benefits from his knowledge depth, teaching style and delivery method.

David holds the Project Management Professional (PMP®)[9] certification from the Project Management Institute (PMI®)[10], a world-wide organization accepted as the industry standard for managing projects as documented in the PMBOK®.

---

[8] "A Guide to the Project Management Body of Knowledge (PMBOK Guide)." Fourth Edition. Project Management Institute, 2008. PMBOK is a trademark of the Project Management Institute, Inc. which is registered in the United States and in other nations.

[9] PMP is a certification mark of the Project Management Institute, Inc. which is registered in the United States and in other nations.

[10] PMI is a service and trademark of the Project Management Institute, Inc. which is registered in the United States and in other nations.

He possesses the Certified Computing Professional designation from the Institute for the Certification of Computing Professionals. The designation is awarded to those individuals who have a wide variety of experience in the IT industry and prove their competencies through a battery of exams. David passed each exam at the Mastery Level.

As a Microsoft Certified Professional in the area of Microsoft Project®, he has written books concerning proper use of MS Project®.

He holds a Master of Science Degree in Computer Science from Purdue University.

David is available for speaking and training opportunities. Contact him at **info@ameagle.com**.

Project Management. It's a career where many are chosen, but few actually chose it.

It is a position where you have one hundred percent of the responsibility and no authority to get the job done.

You manage many people, but none of them report to you and they don't need to listen to you.

It is a job where you'll fail 66% of the time, unless of course, you are managing an IT project where the failure rate zooms to 75% (Standish Group report[11]).

But think about it. If you were a major league baseball player failing only 66% of the times at bat, you'd be worth millions of dollars in salary per year (a 333 batting average), let alone endorsements, speaking engagements and other revenue generating endeavors. Even if you were hitting 250 (failing 75% of the time), you'd still have a six figure income. I would bet, as a project manager, you'd take the six figures and run (pun intended).

Based upon our study[12], eighty percent of project managers are not formally trained in project management. While we are intelligent people with organizational skills, we learn our trade of project management

---

[11] Standish Group. CHAOS original report 1995. CHAOS Summary 2009 Report, April 2009.

[12] American Eagle Group. "A Survey of Project Management Software." May 2007.

through the "school of hard knocks" and by watching others. Of course, they are not formally trained either, so we end up duplicating their bad habits while thinking we are "doing it right." Maybe the lack of formal training in project management has something to do with the high failure rate. In fact, USA companies waste $71 billion annually on failed projects.

The Standish Group's report further details the success rate of those formally trained in project management. It skyrockets to almost 70%—still a 30% failure rate! Are your clients going to permit you to fail 75%, 66% or even 33% of the time? How about repeat business or the possibility of getting referrals?

The good news in all this drudgery is, those in charge of projects are not formally trained either, so they don't know we are failing! There is an old joke about this, "Change the parameters and declare victory. That's how we succeed at project management." Unfortunately, the statement is more fact than fiction.

Creating Successful Projects

For many, project management boils down to managing schedules, budgets and resources. It's about listing all the tasks necessary to complete the project, marshalling the troops to accomplish the tasks and keeping the project under budget.

Project Management Institute (PMI®, at *www.pmi.org*) is an international non-profit which authors the Project Management Body of Knowledge (PMBOK®). According to PMI®, project management is defined as "the application of knowledge, skills, tools and techniques to project activities to meet the project requirements." As you can see, schedules and budgets might be considered tools, but project management requires much more than just the tools.

A project "is a temporary endeavor undertaken to create a unique product, service or result." Temporary means projects have definite begin and end dates; they don't linger forever.

When asked the definition of a successful project, most people say "on time and on budget." Yet when I tell people I can bring any project in "on time and on budget," they simply don't believe me. I assure them I can.

Let's say Bob wants me to build him a boat. He has $250,000 in cash sitting on the table for me to build the boat. I have four weeks to build the boat. Being the smart project manager that I am, I ask some questions to refine the requirements.

PM: "Why four weeks? Why not five weeks?"

Bob: "My brother is coming to visit and I want to show him I am just as successful as he is. He has a boat and I want to show him I can afford one also."

PM: "Ok. If I have to go over $250,000, do I have some flexibility in the budget?"

Bob: "Only if I must stretch beyond that, but I really need to stick close to the $250,000."

PM: "Ok. Thanks."

Four weeks later to the day, I deliver to Bob the nicest looking, made-of-the-finest-quality marine plywood rowboat ever built. On top of that, I only spent $249,000 and returned the balance to Bob. Did I have a successful project?

Most people giggle and say no. Why? I delivered a boat, on time and in this case, under budget. Bob should be thrilled. But he is not because he had expectations and I did not meet them.

A successful project meets or exceeds the expectations of the stakeholders. As consultants who want to excel or be considered excellent, our job is to manage the stakeholder's expectations. Consider the number of stakeholders on any particular project:

- Customers

- Vendors

- Project Sponsor

- Managers

- Executives

- Team Members

- Project Portfolio Managers

- Project Program Managers

- Project Management Office

- Functional Managers

- Operations

- And more. . .

Managing stakeholders' expectations can be daunting, if not impossible to reach. But our success as consultants depends on it.

Education and Process

Since 1969, PMI® has been developing a set of good practices covering the various aspects of a project. Currently, they define forty-two processes in the PMBOK®. These processes guide project activities. When followed, the likelihood of meeting stakeholder expectations rises sharply. Those who study the processes and qualify receive the Project Management Professional (PMP®) certification, recognized world-wide.

The certification and education do not ensure project success, but the project manager is better prepared to conduct the various activities, and learns techniques to manage stakeholders and their expectations better.

This education seems to pay off. According to the Standish Group's report, those trained reach success rates of 70%.

RTMI, Baby

So, the question becomes, why? Why formalize project management? Isn't the Git'r done method good enough? Nights, weekends, whatever it takes, we'll git'r done. How about, "Well, obviously we know what we're doing. We have a multi-billion dollar company here. We must be doing okay." Or, "If it ain't broke, why fix it?" "Besides, all that process stuff simply adds more work, slows things down and no one really looks at it, let alone gives a rat's butt about whether the papers are filled or filed." The answer is simple. RTMI.

RTMI stands for

- Repeatable

- Trackable

- Measureable

- Improvable

Repeatable

Without formalizing our approach to project management, we have a tough time repeating our steps. Decisions made once will be re-made the next time around because we never documented the first one. We have to spend time determining the next steps each time we repeat or do similar tasks. Finally, we have difficulty transitioning our position to someone else because no reference materials exist.

Trackable

Once we can repeat a process, we can track its efficiencies and deficiencies. Tracking is crucial to future improvements. The improvements make the process more efficient and acceptable to customers, managers, executives and other influential stakeholders.

Measureable

By placing tracking points in our processes, we can measure efficiency, proficiency and productivity more easily. We can see bottlenecks, improper practices, and process improvements. We can create measurements where the values provide trends and future states. As we track our practices, we can determine next steps for improvements.

Improvable

After careful consideration, we devise updates to our process, fold them into the flow and repeat the process: repeatable, trackable, measureable and improvable. Without systematizing our practices, we would become rudderless ships wandering in the ocean of projects, never really knowing our direction or destination.

Where Do We Get Started?

So far, we have established several points:

- The majority of projects fail because stakeholder expectations are not met.

- Most project managers are not trained to manage projects properly.

- Trained project managers can reach a success rate of approximately 70%.

- Formalizing our practices so they are repeatable, trackable, measureable, and improvable helps us continually approach higher success rates on projects.

Therefore, the next logical question in our quest to become excellent project managers is where to start?

First, start with yourself. Have you attended a seminar where project management formalization has been taught? It doesn't have to be a five-day, forty-two process, in-depth program which qualifies you to take (and pass) the PMP® exam by PMI®. How about a two-day discussion where an industry recognized methodology is taught with supporting tools such as example project plans, document templates, processes and procedures?

Secondly, does the organization have such material available even though no one uses them? Pull it out, blow off the dust, and crack open the seal. Use templates and forms to get people to provide information—especially stakeholders. If you are required to meet their expectations in order to be successful, then you had better know what their expectations are and how to meet them. Stakeholders are notorious for not providing all their expectations, holding some in reserve. As good project managers, we ask for their expectations, and then ask later on, and again after some time, and so on. Write down their expectations. After time passes, rehearse them with the stakeholders again just to make sure they didn't change or the priorities didn't change.

Triple Constraint – the Trifecta For Success

During your questioning, you are particularly interested in the Triple Constraint. Any project can be defined by the Triple Constraint—Time, Money and Scope. A constraint is anything that binds the activities or options of the team.

Time

Time defines the duration of the project—how long will it take to accomplish the objectives of the project. Usually, stakeholders (especially the influential stakeholders: customers, executives, managers, project sponsor) have an idea how much time they want to spend on this project. It might be expressed in a duration value—10 weeks, 5 months, 2 years. It might be expressed by a single date—April 20th, July 4th.

Certainly, we must understand the stakeholders' expectation around time. Is it flexible? Is it a hard and fast date? If the date can move, can it move only a little or a lot? How was the amount of time derived—a "hard end date," somebody's whim, a Grand Opening, or something else?

Money

How much are the influential stakeholders willing to spend on this project? Is the budget flexible or is there a hard limit? If flexible, by how much?

What happens if there are overruns on resource needs, work not completed or unanticipated circumstances that require more money?

Scope

What exactly is this project supposed to accomplish? What is it not to accomplish? What are the project objectives? Once we meet the objectives, are we finished? What assumptions are being made in order for this project to be viable? What happens if those assumptions are no longer true after a period of time? What becomes of the project? What are the quality requirements of the project's product? What risks might we run into which could delay our progress? These are just a few of the questions you may need to ask to define project scope.

Prioritizing the Triple Constraint

Understanding the Triple Constraint is paramount for any successful project manager. Additionally, he or she needs to understand stakeholder priorities in relationship to each other. The stakeholders will have a driving constraint and a weak constraint. In order to be successful, a project must meet the driving constraint. If it doesn't, no matter what else is done, the project fails.

Driving Constraint

The driving constraint is the one the project manager must meet to be considered successful. Miss this constraint and the project is a failure. Stakeholders' needs are not met. The driving constraints drive the decisions for the project.

Weak Constraint

The weak constraint has the most flexibility. This is the constraint you'll wiggle around on to make adjustments that keep the project on track. Stakeholders have lower expectations on this constraint.

Middle Constraint

The middle constraint is, well… in the middle. It is more flexible than the driving constraint and less flexible than the weak constraint.

As project managers, we do not choose which constraint is weak and which is driving. The stakeholders only reveal the driving and weak constraints after much questioning and discussion. Once set, the project manager had better document them and continually check with the stakeholders about their validity over time. A constraint's priority can and will change.

Using the Triple Constraint to Your Advantage

What's the fuss about the Triple Constraint? Why is it so important? How can we leverage constraints to more effectively manage our projects?

Projects slip-and-slide, ebb-and-flow over time. As the project manager, you must pull levers and push buttons to keep it on course. Using your understanding of the Triple Constraint, you need to know if the scope of the project is more important than the schedule. In other words, if the scope is the driving constraint and time is the weak constraint, then the stakeholder would rather take a bit more time to get the full product as described in the scope. Therefore, when you inform the stakeholders the schedule must slip a bit in order complete the scope, their reaction may be benign compared with how they might react if you tell them you can't complete the project to their specifications.

Since stakeholders like choices and want to feel in control of the decisions, providing options based upon the Triple Constraints goes a long way. Assume time is the weak constraint and scope is the driving constraint. Here are three choices you can offer the stakeholders to meet the project requirements:

- Remove items from the scope to meet the deadline, or

- Add more resources to the project, increasing costs while meeting the objectives of the project within the allotted time, or

- Slip the schedule by X days, maintain budget and fulfill the objectives of the project completely.

Although the stakeholders may not be overly thrilled by these options, they will probably choose the third option, given the Triple Constraint priorities.

As a prudent project manager, you would be wise to revisit the Triple Constraint priorities periodically just in case they might change (and they do change, unfortunately) over time.

Freshen Your Project With Scope

If you are permitted to write only one document on your project, the scope document is the one to write.

The scope document provides the overarching directives of the project. Sections to be included in the scope document are:

- Project Name

- Project Sponsor name and contact information

- Project Manager name and contact information

- Project Description

- Project Objectives

- Project Deliverables

- Project Stakeholders—at least the influential ones

- Project Acceptance Criteria

- Product Acceptance Criteria—product is the result of the project regardless of whether it is a product, service or result; what is the project supposed to produce?

- Assumptions

- Constraints

- Business need for project

- Boundaries—what the project will consider and what it will not

The scope document is the central document for the project. While it may not always be called the "scope" document, it defines the work of the project. Because it is so crucial to the success of the project, the project manager must find it and understand its contents.

What should a project manager do if he or she can't locate it, or worse, he or she is told it doesn't exist? Write one! Take the time to write a scope document using the component list from above. Review it with the stakeholders and get them to agree to its contents. Managing a project without it is like flying in the dark without instruments or lights. You'll get somewhere, but it might be a solid wall of failure.

Common Understanding and Basis for All Project Decisions

Why is the scope document so critical for a project? According to the PMBOK®, it fulfills two primary needs for the project:

1. It provides a common understanding of the project among all the stakeholders, and

2. It is used as the basis for all project decisions.

The project stakeholders relying on the scope document include executives, customers, managers, project team members, vendors, project sponsor, and especially the project manager.

Ideally, all influential stakeholders must sign-off on the document before the project continues. Their signature signifies they have read and understand the project's objectives and deliverables. If anything is missing in the description, it must be added before the project continues. If it contains anything the project is not supposed to accomplish, those items must be removed. Upon signature, the stakeholder agrees the document contains only the work to be accomplished and nothing but the work.

If anything is inadvertently left out of the scope document, it will not be accomplished unless it becomes an approved change to the project.

The scope document is the basis for project decisions. Everyone knows that as projects progress, stakeholders request changes. Those changes will be considered in light of the scope document. If a change fits within the purview of the project as described in the scope, then it will be considered. If it does not fit within the scope, the change is shelved until a later time, for another project, or rejected totally.

Scope Creep

Scope creep is not that little green guy who comes into your office regularly—that's your boss. Scope creep is implementing unapproved changes. If there is only one process you are permitted to implement in the organization, then Change Control with a Change Control Board is it. By rigorously using a change control methodology, a project manager can begin to control scope creep—the #1 reason projects fail.

The Change Control Methodology is used to document changes to the project and understand their impacts to the schedule, budget and resources before changes can be implemented. Hallway Tackles (someone stops the project manager in the hall and requests a change with full expectation it will be done) and Shoulder-Taps (similar to Hallway Tackles, except done by tapping on the shoulder of the project managers while they're in the office or through email, voicemail, or text message) are the common "change control methodologies" in most organizations. The project manager is told of a change and expected to carry it out.

Nibble-Down-The-Lane is another technique for slipping in unbridled changes. In this scheme, someone keeps asking various people on the project team for a change until they get a "yes vote." The project manager is unaware of the change being made until after it is completed, by which time the schedule and budget are blown.

Unfortunately, without formal Change Control, no consideration for the schedule or budget is made. At the end of the project, all stakeholders develop amnesia and forget about the additions and changes requested for the project scope. They ask the poor project manager why the project is over budget and far behind schedule. When the project manager tries to respond, he or she is simply told, "There is no excuse."

In a proper Change Control process, a Change Control Board receives change requests. Each request is documented and tracked. The change request is reviewed to understand the impact it has on the schedule, budget and resources. If the Board decides to implement the change, then the schedule, budget and resources are changed to reflect the impact, and a new date and budget are set.

At the end of the project, when the project manager delivers the project, it is a success if he or she meets the new timeline and costs. Surely, someone will state the project was over budget and behind schedule, but the project manager can proudly pull out the approved change requests to show he or she met project requirements.

Rejected change requests are also documented. They can be used for input into future projects or project phases, or simply dropped. The decision to reject a change request must be documented in case the requestor comes back to understand why.

To be a successful project manager and to control scope creep, insist on a change control methodology. It doesn't have to be complicated, but it does need to exist and be used.

Three Cornerstones To Success

Managing projects is not easy. As a project manager, the odds are against you to deliver successful projects that meet stakeholders' expectations. Many factors are working against you. Knowing these factors exist, you can counter them and improve your chances of delivering a project successfully.

As project managers, we don't have the authority to make sweeping changes within organizations. Ideally, we'd like to develop processes to help us manage the resources, budgets and schedules assigned to us— but even if we had the authority, we don't have the time. Therefore, what three cornerstones can we set in place, given our limited ability to exact change that gives us the biggest bang for our effort?

1. Understand the Triple Constraint

Whether you are in an organization that has a process for everything from making coffee to constructing billion dollar buildings to solving world hunger, or in a company that can't spell process, as a project manager you can ask questions to understand the Triple Constraint for projects you are managing. Understand the Constraints, their priorities and stakeholders' expectations around them.

2. A Solid Scope Document

Develop a scope document using the list of components described earlier in this chapter. It is your "guiding light" to success as you meet the project requirements. It provides a common understanding for all stakeholders and it helps you manage their expectations. If expectations change, the stakeholders will notify you when you periodically review the document with them.

3. Change Control Methodology with Change Control Board

This is your defense against scope creep—your armor against unapproved changes. Without the Change Control Board, change will spread out of control throughout the project, leading to definite failure. The members of the Board can help you keep your project on track because they help guard against unnecessary and counterproductive changes. Implement a change control methodology to increase the likelihood of project success.

Wrapping It Up

Project Management—a career where many are chosen. It doesn't have to be one with a high failure rate. RTMI your projects—repeatable, trackable, measureable, and improvable. RTMI your cornerstones and you'll be surprised how much better you can manage projects.

Project Communications for Senior Consultants

--------‚■■■‚--------

Steve Backman

Steve has nearly thirty years of experience with software development and technology strategy. Steve gained professional experience in corporate software development and was intrigued by emerging standards for cost-effective and forward-looking database systems. He launched Database Designs in 1989 to bring emerging new perspectives to nonprofit and public sector organizational processes. He chose to keep the company small, independent, and focused on providing select clients comprehensive support for unique and creative solutions to strategic challenges.

Steve's consulting group prides itself on being platform independent, advising, implementing, and integrating both the latest Microsoft .Net® web technologies as well as Drupal® and other Open Source environments. The group's approach is to blend and integrate off-the-shelf commercial and Open Source systems with independently developed tools and techniques.

With liberal arts degrees from Harvard and Yale, Steve turned to political activism in Boston grass roots causes in the 1970s. He later brought his "organizer's mentality" to technology strategy and systems consulting. Steve speaks and writes frequently, particularly on technology issues for nonprofits.

These days, it's hard to advance your consulting practice without careful consideration of your communication tools. It wasn't always so. Classic books about success as a computer technology consultant offer advice about marketing, preparing proposals, managing your work and in general staying organized. They rarely get down to effective tools.

This may seem strange, since so much of what we do involves advising others on systems and solutions. The fact is, over the last several years, the range and power of communication tools that truly aid project work have grown considerably. The price and pain of getting started or professionalizing your techniques have dropped. It's safe to say *email + attachments* no longer represents a viable strategy.

We are surrounded by technology-rich communications in our business lives. Our clients expect us to use professional-grade communications tools at least up to the standard they encounter elsewhere.

As a consultant, your communication tools and personal infrastructure are likely to build over time. Yet hardly anything else you can establish will more strongly affect your week to week satisfaction and success. Let's take a look at some choices in key priority areas.

My primary focus here is simple: Support current clients and projects first. Devote time to outreach and marketing tools second.

For consultants, business and personal success depends on successful execution of critical projects. Many consultants start out with a reputation for solid work and expertise, coupled with unevenness in providing good communication. In the beginning, it seems like all that really matters is getting the work done. But in the long run, building a consulting practice depends on repeat business and work of mouth. For this, the quality, ease and professionalism of your project communication matter.

Project Management and Communication Systems

There is no perfect set of tools for project communications. What you need will reflect critical determinants of how you work. Accept that you must go through a period of experimentation. Try out new tools on personal or *pro bono* projects first, so you can assess what fits without the pressures of project success.

I intentionally refer to project communications and not project management. Traditionally, they were one and the same. Project management meant Microsoft Project®, Gantt charts and other formal means for scheduling, scoping, assigning specific responsibilities, and determining task dependencies.

These can bring essential discipline to a project. Yet reviewers of project management success or failure increasingly emphasize factors that may lie orthogonal to formal organizational tools. Effective stakeholder involvement is one, as David Zimmer emphasizes in the previous chapter.

A core theme in Scott Berkum's powerful book "The Art of Project Management"[13] is that project success depends as much on the communications that occur during the inevitable crises over cost, schedule, or features as it does on the formal tracking tools you use to ward off crises.

Meanwhile, alongside the maturation of such products as Microsoft Project® in the 1990s, Lotus Notes® (now owned by IBM®) pioneered corporate "groupware." Since that wave of innovation, Web 2.0 and social media systems arose. All of these encourage collaborative free-flowing discussion. They don't contain a backbone structure to aid and abet successful projects.

Somewhere in the middle lies adoption and customization of structured project communications systems. These systems surround formal project documentation with equally formalized ways of fostering and organizing discussion to produce timely, successful planning and execution. These emerged alongside new thinking about project effectiveness. The more your projects focus on general technology strategy, the more true this will be.

The Importance of Client-Side Project Communications

Distinguishing project communications from project management leads to a second point: we need to separate client-side from consultant-side project communication strategies.

Client-side communications refers to all the joint-team interactions that have to do with scoping, scheduling, planning, strategizing, and advising. If the project includes implementation of a system, client-side communications also includes designing, reviewing, testing, migrating data, and releasing. My experience is that project success generally depends most on the timeliness and richness of client participation in planning and discussion—not just at the beginning, but throughout the project.

Consultant-side communications refers to the more detailed technical preparation of specifications and tracking of work. While coordinating your own team also takes patience and effort, chances are that your team will have a higher threshold of pain.

---

[13] Berkun, Scott. "The Art of Project Management: Theory in Practice." O'Reilly Media, Inc. April 21, 2005.

There are certainly exceptions. First team projects or collaboration among several consulting teams present special challenges. Overall, you may get by with *ad hoc* communications or need more rigorous technical tools for consultant side collaboration.

Whatever the size of a project, the more it focuses on strategy, analysis and planning, the more important it is to first get client-side communications right. This applies regardless of whether or not you also need traditional project management apparatus.

Similarly, the more heterogeneous the client team is, the more you need tools with the least friction for user involvement and engagement. *Heterogeneous* in this context refers to the mix of technical people with non-technical product and program managers, executive sponsors, and other senior advisors.

If you truly expect to have senior management involved outside of face to face meetings, your tools need an ease and fluidity that will draw management in to key decision points. This is true whether you work with very large corporations or small to medium businesses and nonprofits.

Six elements of effective client side project communications stand out. You can address those elements one by one, to the degree they fit your work. You need to set a pattern that truly fits the type of projects and style of consulting you do. If you adopt any of the popular systems out there today, you will find hints and suggestions for how to organize your work. Yet corralling a set of tools doesn't ensure great project management. Project communication tools underlie, support, and ease successful project management—they don't ensure it. Consider how these six blend to support your practice, and then look for what fits.

Support Effective Discussion with a Project Blog

Computer technology projects need continuous collaborative discussion, from beginning to end. Scoping, strategizing, planning, designing, executing, reviewing, refining, preparing, documenting, and releasing all have strong conversational elements. A consultant needs a steady means for engaging the client and other consulting team members throughout the project. While messaging choices abound, in today's modern era, a private project blog is likely to provide the best support. If you do nothing else in the way of formal project communication tools, consider setting up a private blog for each new project.

Even if your team members don't blog themselves, they probably read blog posts, and understand the metaphors of comments and responses to posts. This is easy to settle into, no matter what your technical level. Though a project blog may sound odd at first, it compares well with two competing older ideas: relying on email, and setting up a bulletin board or forum.

The blog itself as a technology is not the point. Enshrining the lively blog style of discussion in your projects should be your goal. What makes up this style of communication?

- A familiar, intuitive way to write, edit and post messages. Blogs typically work with plain text, or at most with lightweight formatting. You want to reduce all technical barriers to engaging all team members taking part right from the beginning.

- A permanent, shared repository of all project discussion in one place. You can't count on this by only using a group email list.

- A searchable, categorizable repository of project discussion. More important than providing free-form text search, blogs imply the ability to categorize or tag messages. Blogs help team members locate important discussion threads, and they facilitate a shared lexicon of project terms and phrases. When issues arise, everyone—client and consultant—can find the same information in the same way.

- Multiple means to stay in touch. A blog can be a private, "members only" web site, which all team members can reach anywhere they can get on the web. Project blogs also should allow subscription via RSS news feed or email. Look for the ability to respond to messages from within email, yet see them collected in a project news/message/blog page. Because the delivery medium can vary, you reduce the likelihood of team members missing important messages.

- Optional ability to direct discussion to particular team members. The blog belongs to a project, yet depending on the size and diverse roles of team members, you may want to be able to target some notifications to a subset of the overall team.

You definitely want to move beyond relying on email. Consulting projects typically shape up through email, punctuated by phone and in-person meetings. If you don't take care, the project will settle into a groove of email exchange. Email today has the advantage of pervasiveness. It is a tried and true communications medium predating the World Wide Web. Yet email is messy, individualized and less collaborative in comparison with the modern blog format.

Likewise, we have all experienced older-style forum or bulletin board formats for interactive discussion. These continue in the world of product self-help pages. When I hear a suggestion to set up a forum or bulletin board for project planning discussion, I feel a collective drawing-back as team members remember frustrated experiences trying to figure out through a forum why this or that product doesn't work. Bulletin boards require more clicks and maneuvering to find what you want, and offer less freedom in organizing and categorizing discussion. Avoid them for your projects.

You can easily create a private standalone blog site for a project. Most modern project communications software relies upon this metaphor for collaborative discussion, and not traditional forums.

Translating Project Scope into Shared Calendar and Task Lists

Translating a work agreement into a practical organizational framework is a key challenge in every project. Sometimes the agreed-upon scope naturally flows into a schedule of work and deliverables. You may be blessed with projects where once the scope is set, emailing everyone a spreadsheet or other project schedule chart to have and to hold will do.

Often, adjustments occur, both at the outset and along the way. Where there is room for adjustment, ultimate project success may depend on communications transparency and collaboration. Everyone should see the calendar and associated tasks in real time, without room for ambiguity, and with clear assignment of responsibility from start to end.

Formal project management tools may help the experienced consultant to set out task dependencies and such. These may work just fine within the ranks of an experienced consulting team, but frequently break down where client responsibilities mingle with consultant responsibilities. To have a successful review cycle, for example, the consultant needs to be sure the client knows new material is ready to review, and the client needs to know when, where and how to provide their responses. It is easy to slip a week or two on mismatched communications.

Modern technology projects need and can easily have shared calendars for major milestone events. The art of this for a consultant is that you are not going to want to use the client's internal calendar, since you have your own. Likewise, putting a mob of people on your own calendar rarely makes sense.

A project calendar can be as simple as creating a shared Google™ calendar. Alternatively, a project calendar can be part of a larger arena: grouping the major expectations for each milestone event into collaborative task lists.

To-do or task lists organize the distinct steps for achieving success in a project. For effective client-side communication, an experienced consultant wants a clear, transparent, broadly assessable means to organize the main tasks and phases of a project. If you want to be able to assign tasks to client team members, you need this.

A to-do list mostly assigns responsibilities, checks them off as they get done, and bundles them up toward project milestones that should correspond to your statement of work. You have to find your way as to how much complexity you need. Do you need to focus on the one person chiefly responsible for completion of a task, or do you need to assign a team? Do you need start and end dates for individual items, or just for the set of items that comprise a project deadline? Do you need to set priorities, indicate level of effort required, or categorize the type of work to address the issue?

These extra refinements are not necessarily bad. Just note that each layer of optional features may reduce participation by non-technical members of your team. These features typically come in issue tracker systems. If you really need these things, you need a tool that reflects them. If you don't really need them, having them as options on each task entry may just create project communications noise.

From the client-side communications point of view, I can't emphasize enough how important it is for the entire client team to be able to regularly see a simple list of the elements in a project phase. The chief client representatives want to know who is in charge of each measurable item, and what is going to get done overall this month or this phase. They want to know, "How much closer to done overall are we, and can I tell on my own without asking the consultant?" They may not want to get much deeper in order to make their own effective reports to senior management.

Clients Track Tasks, Consultants Track "Bugs" and "Issues"

Don't put overall project tasks and milestones in a "bug tracker."

Much to the initial frustration of software developers, a to-do list is not a software bug tracker. When projects involve developing complex software, you probably need issue tracking as well, with the features suggested above. You may find that in the planning and early implementation phases, an easy to understand calendar and associated task lists make the most sense. When a new software system or infrastructure upgrade nears roll-out, you may need the granularity of bug tracking or issue tracking.

For example, if the week's work depends on a client analyst sending along sample data or a product manager providing comments on a specification, it is not particularly friendly to record that task as a "bug" or "issue." If all you have is the issue tracker, with all its formalities, the client side of your team is likely to fall back on email messages—or you may wait longer than expected for a response.

Here's one way to think of the difference. A task list associated with a calendar date ought to point back to the original scope of work. This is an important early warning system with regard to scope creep or milestone slippage. By contrast, a bug tracker should be focused and specific, with prioritization by the client and time estimates and assignment to engineering to ensure a successful launch.

Personal Calendar and Tasks

Don't count on using project calendar and tasks for your overall calendar and tasks.

Having focused on a project communications system, you may wonder if the calendar and task management there can satisfy all your needs for overall task management as well. Busy, more experienced consultants should not count on it. A senior computer consultant working on his or her own or in a consulting practice generally will need a higher level of self-discipline about schedule and tasks than other professionals. It is worth the time to find tools to support that requirement.

Even though it goes against the grain, I find myself making peace with multiple, overlapping systems for managing contact and task information in more than one place. Part of my work involves advising clients on how to reduce that kind redundancy. Yet reducing or eliminating it bears a cost. Starting out, consultants tend to be somewhat *ad hoc*. Gaining experience, it becomes important to look for effective communications with the least overall overhead for yourself, even if this means some redundancy in information management.

I find that I have weekly and daily priorities that don't fit neatly into the client-project-due date-task hierarchy of a project management system. Disciplining myself to write things down on more than scraps of paper requires having a personal dashboard that lets me record everything in the same fashion and focus on major priorities.

I'm going to say it—there is nothing wrong with a notebook, pen and paper calendar if you can make it work for you. I have a small pocket notebook with me at all times. I generally find it less off-putting than having a computer open in a client meeting. Later, to avoid losing track, everything goes into an electronic task list or memo. In figuring out what works for you, focus in on these features:

- Where do you need to see your personal tasks? Just once a day and then on paper? Or on the move on your laptop, PDA or the web? This depends on you—where you typically work, how much you are on the road, and what you like to have with you.

- Do you need to see tasks on an electronic calendar? Some communications tools provide an RSS or other data "feed" into your calendar alongside the tasks you add on your own.

- How much time do you want to put into categorizing, prioritizing, and labeling your tasks, as opposed to just listing them?

- Do you need anyone else to see and help maintain your task list?

For some of us, monitoring personal tasks involves a philosophy or methodology. David Allen's "Getting Things Done" [14] is a popular example of such a system, and there are inserts to Microsoft Outlook® or Google™ applications that support it. Do you want to impose such a discipline on your calendar, email and task list? I can't fully live the GTD way, but I have adopted elements of it and value its integration with my daily routine.

Some consultants put a high priority on integrating task management with a consultant services time and billing system. Good advice would be to make sure you can stay on top of your work and calendar first, and if this means re-entering your billable time separately, it's worth it. As the world of web services continues to evolve, project task-and-billing systems are emerging in some project software today, and may become more easily integrated with your favorite tools.

Document Repository

Projects have a significant body of spreadsheets, word processing documents, mockup images and more. Each project should have file space. Members of a team may think in spreadsheets, charts, slide shows, or entity relationship diagrams, not to mention word processing documents, and you need a place to put them. If email is not the best way to organize discussion, email attachments as your document repository certainly also falls short.

Internal corporate projects may have the luxury of just designating network directories to hold documents. An outside consultant may or may not

---

[14] Allen, David. "Getting Things Done: The Art of Stress-Free Productivity." Penguin, December 31, 2002.

easily gain access to those directories. Even if the client is willing to do this, I find that it often adds friction to the project. You are dependent on a network administrator to determine who can read and write files, when, and where.

There are ways to set up secure, shared web storage for a project and host your document repository there. Many consultants set up private, compartmentalized space on their web site for this. Web sites built with contemporary content management systems, both commercial and open source, make this straightforward.

I find it more professional to use the document repository provided by a complete, integrated project communication system. Separating the hosted project repository from the consultant's own web site helps ensure buy-in. Psychologically, this step places the important documents of a project on neutral ground for both client and consultant. If you need to bring in specialists for certain phases of a project, you can add them quickly and easily. These systems are likely to offer versioning and revision tracking that can help in refining planning documents.

Ideally, the document repository should have organizational features. All the planning material for a certain phase of work should be collected together. When the next phase starts, you should be able to have a clean space to put the next round of materials.

Project Memos

While a document repository is essential, for formulating key project documents requiring sign-off, I find it invaluable to keep a set of simple clear memos which live directly on the project web site. This is often the best way to collaboratively formulate anything from an important meeting agenda to the prioritized features for a software release.

When you use a document repository, editing takes place offline. Individuals upload and download documents (ideally one person at time), and let everyone know when they are finished. By contrast, a shared memo page is edited directly on the web site.

Adding collaborators to a shared Google™ doc is a readily available way to experience the power of this type of communication device. Having a collaboratively edited memo pad open for notes during a meeting or phone call can be confusing, distracting and anarchic. Nevertheless, it can also be invaluable in getting ideas out and building consensus.

Modern project communication systems offer their equivalents embedded in the project space. Look for a system that can track revisions to memos so the course of a discussion can be checked.

I find these shared notepads essential in collaboratively defining both high level policy statements and detailed specifications for a data or web system. Although a picture (such as a mockup, flow chart, or spreadsheet) may be worth a thousand words, it is important to get sign-off on simple text specification of goals and features. If you are using a formal technology planning discipline, these notepads could be the place for "user stories" and the like.

Private wikis, popularized by Wikipedia®, sometimes get used in this way. I find that a wiki may provide a useful way for a technical team to begin and grow a documentation project. I don't find them as useful as a means of collaboratively editing important project documents.

For internal planning and a first-time team of people who are not especially technical, using a wiki requires a period of acclimatization. Technical people may insist the wiki framework offers simple elegance. Don't believe it. For writing, outlining, commenting and editing, the wiki world is alien enough that you cannot assume spontaneous adoption and usage. Until you get used to it (which may be the week after your first project milestone date), using a markup language that is anything but "what you see is what you get" (WYSIWYG) and the wiki method for connecting pages will hold back the free flow of ideas and discussion.

Spending time teaching it may be useful for a technical team constructing a large manual or resource guide. It may not be worth it for a client-consultant team that needs to reach important strategic consensus. Communication tools that work from a more blog-like metaphor may seem more familiar and engage a diverse user base more quickly.

Some project communication system "memo" or "writeboard" features may use familiar WYSIWYG formatting, and others use wiki-like mark-up language. The difference is that they don't depend on wiki formatting and page linking conventions. The pages should gain the same categorization, organizational structure and visual presentation that other elements of the project have so everyone can just review, comment and edit.

Informal Chat and Discussion Channel

Another element to consider is a private *ad hoc* means for team members to communicate instantaneously on daily work.

"The review data only includes current FY projections. Who can help me get the rest today for tomorrow's presentation?" If I have to start calling or emailing, the afternoon may be gone. If I can post a message to whoever is on the team and "listening," someone might respond in minutes.

This is the instantaneous, continuous communication style popularized in social media. A distributed, geographically spread, time zone challenged team may well benefit at some points in a project from having quick way to hold a group chat. While group chat via Internet Relay Chat (IRC) has been around for a long, long time, such older technical tools are not nearly as intuitive as having, say, a private Twitter channel or open Skype line. Some systems offer that kind of channel, standalone or as part of a project suite. You may find it handy.

Getting What You Need Today

The common theme here is reducing the barrier to collaborative discussion, and maximizing its positive contribution to project success. Clay Shirky's ground-breaking book "Here Comes Everybody"[15] opens up the world of collaborative action now energized by new technologies. Successful consultants implicitly know they need to work collaboratively to ensure project success. The right tools can make a difference.

You can certainly find your own path to one or more of the priority communication requirements discussed here. In recent years, a class of software systems, primarily web hosted, have arisen which group together suites of tools to meet this collaborative project communications challenge.

You may find that different projects require different emphases. As a senior consultant, you will want to orient, adapt, or customize a system to fit with your own professional style. This is more than just "branding" a tool. If you don't want to get needlessly bogged down in details, you should think in terms of evaluating and adopting a software tool specifically targeted to project communications. This will make more sense for a busy, senior consultant than either using generic groupware tools or cobbling together a series of *ad hoc* or home grown favorites.

As I write this in 2009, most of this class of software comes as Software as a Service (SaaS). Set up an account in 5 minutes, and let it grow or shrink month to month. Some are installable on your own servers, and some are Open Source. For the popular subscription model SaaS packages, the more projects you have, the more you spend per month. In evaluating what you need, weigh these business considerations alongside the communications features described above.

---

[15] Shirky, Clay. "Here Comes Everybody: The Power of Organizing Without Organizations." Penguin, February 24, 2009.

Some examples worth considering today are:

- BasecampHQ (***www.37Signals.com***)

- Central Desktop

- ActiveCollab

- Zoho

- Open Atrium

I would steer away from general groupware tools like Sharepoint®, as this requires too much configuration to get what you want. On the other hand, enterprise suites like Salesforce® and NetSuite®, supplemented with project communication add-ons, may make sense for large projects with a single corporate or organizational entity. No doubt the lineup will change with time, but whatever comes will probably build on these new ways of organizing project work.

Aside from evaluating communication requirements against your type of projects, you also need to take into account the business side of choosing the right tools.

Here are some questions to ask, oriented for the independent consultant, in addition to evaluating the features described above:

- Is your workload a series of smaller engagements? Look for features and pricing that fit better with lots of engagements and points of contact at once.

- How big and varied do you expect your project teams to be? Do you require extensive collaboration with others, or mostly work on your own?

- How easy will it be to pull out all your project history in standard format? How easy will it be to archive all the documents when a project winds down? This is more of an issue with hosted software, and can even be an issue with software you install yourself.

- In a related vein, how do you and your clients interpret security and confidentiality issues? What can you learn about the stability and future path of the vendor? For some consultants, these considerations may point toward commercial grade hosted software, with encrypted web pages. For others, it may point toward licensed or open source software, locally installed and controlled.

- How flexible is the software in adding and compartmentalizing users? Traditional tools tend to operate from the viewpoint of a single corporate entity. Even if they support multiple simultaneous projects, they tend to assume a single category of participants. Independent consultants generally need a system where you can securely compartmentalize different client companies and projects, as well as preserve an archive of useful materials to draw upon. As you define a project, you want to be able to add one or more companies in addition to your own, and one or more users from each of those companies. For projects of limited time duration, you generally do not want to use software that requires per-user licensing fees or complex registration and authentication.

- What should you do to round out your portfolio of tools for organizing work?

- Does the system have a look, professionalism and ability to "brand" commensurate with the way you want to work?

- Do the payment terms work well for you now and offer the ability to flexibly gear up or down over time?

- Do you need to integrate technical documentation as well—flow charts, page mockups and designs, Gantt charts, network diagrams, database entity relationship diagrams? Does the tool include them (not likely), or can you incorporate them easily?

A Word About Managing Your General Contact List

While current clients take center stage, consultants also need to steadily build up a larger contact list. All your tools together should support collecting and refining a useful, focused overall contact list in one place, whether that one place is a formal contact relationship manager (CRM) or just your email address book. As with personal task management, you may be tempted to use the contact lists you build up in your project communications systems. Here again, I counsel getting the project communications right, and when the time comes focus on your overall contact list separately. If they happen to coincide, great, but don't count on it.

Does this mean you need to license Customer or Contact Relationship Management Software? Salesforce, NetSuite and other major players have gained traction by providing a more holistic and integrated view of your business contacts. These may offer the opportunity to add general or industry-specific project tracking along the side. Beginning consultants probably don't need or want the overhead involved in this kind of intensive tracking. Solo practitioners, beginning or advanced, may not see the point to it. Many consultants and other professionals today do all their general contact management through professional networking services such as LinkedIn. These services increasingly offer tie-ins with outreach and marketing activity.

That said, as the power and ease of use of CRM software grows, it may make sense to take a look. As with the project communications tools described above, using a formal system may add the layer of regularity and professionalism you need to cultivate in your relationships. This is especially so if you work in a team. Here are several reasons to consider adopting a CRM framework, even if it means duplicating the user lists you keep in project communications software:

- You will gain a centralized, web-based address book accessible anywhere you are, whether or not you have your own laptop with you.

- There are important advantages to separating your general contact list from project team members. Not everyone on project teams wants to or should get your general consultant messages.

- You will be able to manage searchable, reportable tasks; remember phone calls and meetings; organize documents and streams of notes all in one place. It will help you keep marketing opportunities and current client communication in sync. Some systems emphasize a refreshing, enticing Web 2.0 interface that makes you want to sit down and review your priority business development and other opportunities. Others emphasize comprehensive tracking and reporting.

- You may achieve the Nirvana of integration with your calendar, email software, smartphone and almost anything else with the least of headaches.

- You can assure yourself of reliable, continuous off-site back-up of that precious commodity: your cumulative address book and memory of contact. How many of us have endured painful loss from corruption of our email address book and email files?

- You may really want the peace of mind of cross platform convenience. A web-based system means you don't have to worry if you decide to move from Windows to a Mac or beyond.

- A CRM system may also have a close relationship with an email broadcast or newsletter tool, or contact forms on your web site. At some point, every experienced consultant faces a decision about whether to put time and effort into an email newsletter, alert, content bulletin or other regular outbound message system. These days, a regular blog can be a suitable alternative for some, and there are many other opportunities for regularly reaching targeted audiences.

The strategies involved are beyond the scope of this discussion, which focuses on communications tools *per se*. The important point is that the cost, time requirements, and payoff in messaging by using a professional email broadcast tool have grown, and the penalties for relying on older-style group email lists such as in Microsoft Outlook® have grown.

Final Thoughts

The philosophical bent of this discussion reflects my experience. Yes, I focus on making the client side of project communications engaging, collaborative and inclusive. While it guarantees nothing, it seems to offer the best foundation for success. This perspective does require changes in thinking.

It requires living more on the web than I used to, and that implies coming to terms with security, back-up, and confidentiality in new ways. The truth is, we all have to think differently about this whether it's a matter of using services out there "in the cloud" or letting clients onto trusted private internal networks.

It means thinking differently about hardware. These days, my trusty yet heavy notebook sits on my desk most of the time, and I go through the day with a lightweight netbook that gets me on the web or into other remote services. It means doing more on mobile device as well.

I accept that not everything lives in one system. Efficiency in time and communication right now does seem to mean using different systems and databases for different things, and I can live with that.

What matters is that I use the project communication tools currently best suited to the needs of my clients, my teams and myself. That will be as true tomorrow as it is today, and it will remain true no matter how much the tools change.

Getting Off the Clock

Randy Hayman

Randy started his first successful independent consulting business in 1999, with a partner whom he bought out in 2004. PureIce, Inc. was created as a time and materials based practice. Randy grew the business, adding employees and subcontractors, only to find the employee mentoring he did was so successful that all of the employees eventually resigned to do their own thing.

In 2004, Randy partnered with another entrepreneur and started a business on a fixed priced model, providing high value custom packaged solutions. Ethereal Media Group, Inc. was created to remove end user complexity from integration of emerging technologies.

Randy continues to spend his time working with both of these companies. In his spare time, Randy stays current with emerging technologies, best practices, networking and security, enabling him to solve challenging problems with just the right amount of technology.

The Cost of Doing Business

Know Your Costs in Excruciating Detail

To determine whether your value package is aligned with the business value your clients may receive from your product and services, you need to calculate your Cost of Doing Business and the minimum price you need to charge for your value package to meet your business revenue goals.

In order to find your cost of doing business, calculate your theoretical hourly rate and expenses. You can do this easily by the following method:

First, calculate a realistic utilization for yourself (and your employees).

For example, 100% utilization = 8 hours/day * (261 weekdays in 2009) = 2088 hours maximum.

Utilization overhead = all non-billable hours such as vacation, holiday, bench, business administration, sales and marketing, networking, professional development, pro-bono work, etc.

Subtract the utilization overhead from 2088 hours to find your theoretical utilization in hours. Divide your theoretical utilization hours by 2088 to determine your projected utilization percentage.

Second, calculate realistic business expenses for the business per year for your type of business in your jurisdiction.

Determine the salaries, FICA payments, Social Security payments, other business-paid taxes, payroll, insurance (such as life, health, disability, workers compensation, liability, Errors and Omissions, unemployment, automobile), services, business-funded retirement plans, bonuses, distributions, automobile expenses (such as parking, mileage, lease payments), meals and entertainment, equipment purchases or leases, professional development (such as dues and subscriptions, business partner programs, books, training, seminars, conferences including registration, travel, hotels), business communications (such as DSL or cable broadband, ISP, web hosting, cell phones, data plans, fax or landline), electricity, rent, supplies (office and other), software licensing and maintenance fees, postage, order fulfillment, accounting, legal, research and development, business reinvestment funds, marketing, collateral costs, and so on.

Your theoretical hourly rate for the year is the realistic business expenses sum per year divided by your theoretical utilization in hours.

Putting all of these numbers into a spreadsheet will allow you to perform what-if scenarios. See Figure 1 for an example spreadsheet.

As we shall see later, knowing your theoretical hourly rate is part of your value pricing strategy.

Time & Materials vs. Fixed Pricing

As you can see from the previous exercise, the hourly time and materials business model is extremely sensitive to the number of hours billed and the billing rate—if you want to earn more, work more hours or raise your rates.

Figure 1 Cost of Doing Business Spreadsheet

2009 Holiday and Time-Off Schedule

Month (2009)	Billable Days	Holidays & Vacation	Holiday Name & Notes
Jan	22	2	New Years Day (1), MLK Jr (19)
Feb	20	1	President's Day (16)
Mar	22	0	
Apr	22	0	
May	21	1	Memorial Day (25)
Jun	22	0	
Jul	23	1	Independence Day Friday 3rd
Aug	21	0	
Sep	22	1	Labor Day (7)
Oct	22	0	
Nov	21	2	Thanksgiving (26 + 27)
Dec	23	2	Christmas (24 + 25)
totals	261	10	
	251		personal day (i.e. Thursday 2 July); max billable days if no vacation
		14	planned non-billable days
BASE-d	237		projected billable days for 2009
BASE-h	1896		billable hours BASE (hourly rates are based on this goal)
100%	2088		
90.8%	1896		If this number goes down, your rate needs to go up to meet expectations & vice versa

Cost of Doing Business as Company

Item	Hourly Cost
Payroll	$65.60
Expenses	$16.60
Business Investment	$13.20
hourly rate needed to meet expectations	$95.40

Business Investment per Employee, assume 1

Item	Annum	Hourly*	
Savings	$0.00	$0.00	
Retirement Plan	$25,000.00	$13.20	25% gross wages
total	$25,000.00	$13.20	

$180,878.40 gross income

Payroll

Item	Annum	Hourly*	
Salary	$100,000.00	$52.80	
Family Health Benefits	$6,222.00	$3.30	~511.10/mo
Est. Tax/Liability	$18,000.00	$9.50	18.00%
total	$124,222.00	$65.60	

Expenses per Employee, assume 1

Item	Annum	Hourly*
Automobile	$2,400.00	$1.30
Meals & Ent	$2,000.00	$1.10
Software & Equipment	$5,000.00	$2.70
PD: Books	$500.00	$0.30
PD: Travel	$1,500.00	$0.80
PD: Per Diem	$3,500.00	$1.90
PD: Registration	$3,000.00	$1.60
Office Utilities**	$3,600.00	$1.90
Office Rent	$0.00	$0.00
Office Supplies	$1,200.00	$0.70

Business Expenses

Item	Annum	Hourly*
Outside Accounting / Tax Prep. etc.	$1,600.00	$0.90
Legal advice, retainer, etc.	$2,400.00	$1.30
Marketing Collateral	$1,200.00	$0.70
Insurance (E&O, GL, Workman's Comp, etc.)	$3,400.00	$1.80
total	$31,300.00	$16.60

INSTRUCTIONS:

Enter your values into any cell that has bold numeric data, the hourly rate (cell I7) is your cost of doing business

This spreadsheet is an example of how one can manage one's own budget, please consult expert advise for your personal situation.

*hourly rates (using annum [N6] / BASE-h [C21]) are rounded up to the next dime, actual totals will sum to less due to this rounding

**Office Utilities: cell phones, phone service, electric, DSL, ...

US Tax liabilities: Fed	State
Withholding	Withholding
Medicare Company	Unemployment
Medicare Employee	Other - e.g. Business Revenue Gross Tier Tax
SS Company	
SS Employee	
Unemployment	

This is a Key Learning: To "Get Off the Clock" and unleash your earning potential, as well as set yourself apart from the commoditized market for ordinary contract labor, you need to break away from the time and materials model.

Value

To establish your value proposition, you must ask, "What's in it for me?" from your prospective client's view. Will engaging you save time for your client, lessen discomfort, increase efficiencies, enable new business, or something else?

Let's say that you custom design and integrate whole house audio/video entertainment systems, home automation, and home networks. The client is likely to be looking for one or more of these products already. However, there are tens (if not hundreds) of businesses in your market area that say they can offer the same or similar services.

Never compete on price. Compete on value and expertise in an integrated solution.

There really is nothing new about what we do. To succeed, you need to provide greater value than your competition. That value may be in better service, more pleasant staff, more intuitive interfaces, or reducing the headaches of your prospective customers and thereby turning them into clients.

Find your competitive niche. Identify exactly what products and services you provide. If the client wants something you don't provide, offer to find a provider and maintain your client relationship by bringing that provider in as a business partner for this job. Then, if it turns out well, make this business partner's services part of your offerings. Doing this demonstrates the added value you provide.

For example, in this custom entertainment system business, do you pull your own wiring to each of the audio, video, and lighting zones, or do you hire electricians to pull the wiring for you? Electricians have the right licensing and tools. They have lots of experience doing this type of work, and they do it very well, so you may not want to compete (on time and materials) with them. Add their services to your package.

Does setting up virtual LANs for different types of networks and securely integrating them give you hives? Find a competent business partner that lives and breathes networking—you add value and expertise to your package offerings.

What other subcontractors might you include in your package? The fact that you *can* do something doesn't necessarily mean that you *should* do it if you can find high quality business partners.

This is a Key Learning: Once you have determined your competitive niche, expand it with business partners. Doing it all yourself may be limiting your earning potential or diluting your expertise.

In this theoretical custom entertainment systems business, here's an example of adding more value in the eyes of the client. When you get your initial consultation or walk-through opportunity with the client, identify what they are looking for, educate them on what technology is available to them, how you can hide the system complexity, how you can make their house come alive with music and/or video solutions in a manner that they can simply and easily control wherever they are. Demonstrate your expertise by listening and offering advice on all of the options that fit the client's needs.

Tell the client that you have partnered with excellent electricians to do any in-wall and in-ceiling work needed with minimal disruption to their home and to them as a family.

Tell the client that you will also provide a secure home network that integrates their music library with the new home entertainment systems, and that you can provide remote management and monitoring of the home entertainment systems as an added service. In this manner, you can demonstrate your added value by identifying problems with the system before the client is aware of the problem.

Tell the client that part of your service is to provide training on and documentation of their new system upon completion and two weeks after that, and again two weeks after that as they grow accustomed to their new systems.

You might want to mention that you are not the lowest cost provider in this market, but you are the highest value provider, installing what the client wants in a highly intuitive manner. For example, tell them that a key to this is the touch points to the system. If they are going to spend a significant amount of money on a whole house entertainment system, they need to spend enough money to get high quality programmable remote controls: both handheld and in-wall units that will allow them to use the system in a manner they choose, not in a manner that is dictated to them by less capable remote controls.

You might also mention how your custom programming will allow them to use the system easily. Describe a real world situation for them. For example, tell them that when they sit down to watch a movie, they can press one button on their handheld remote and it will turn the TV, movie library, and audio video receiver on, set the volume to a predetermined level, turn down the lights, and take them to the on-screen menu that allows them to select which movie to watch. They can then easily navigate to the movie they want to watch. When they need to take a break, another button pauses the movie and brings the lights up enough just for them to see. Press that button again, and the lights go back down and the movie resumes. Ask the client to describe how they think they'll use their new system and how they use their existing systems to get other real world scenarios, and document them.

Mention that there are a plethora of new ways to use their television with this new system. If they want to order movies online, that can be integrated into the system. If they want to buy songs online, you can add that. If they want to check the local weather or the weather at their vacation place, you can add that also—and it can all be done from their television viewing chair without a keyboard or mouse or even sitting down at their computer.

Talk to the client in their terms about the relative complexity of what your work entails to get all of the pieces talking to each other seamlessly, and you will further demonstrate your value.

When you are done with the walk-through, thank the potential client for their time and tell them when you will get back to them with a preliminary design. Don't miss that deadline—it is the initial impression of your worthiness to be taken at your word.

As you and the client go back and forth working out details of the design and placement of devices, provide guidance and advice to help the client make better decisions.

Look at all the ways you have shown the client your added value: You provide expert solutions design, all wiring, all installation, an improved network, remote management, custom programming of the remotes, training and documentation, all with professionalism typically not found among your competitors.

Pricing Your Product/Service as a Package

In this hypothetical home entertainment business, once the design work is complete, you have a list of materials and services you will provide—an item by item listing of absolutely everything—down to the terminations for every cable and wire. You also have a CAD-style diagram of the home showing which device goes where. You need to know your costs to effectively price your package, but you need to price your package at the value level, not your time and materials level.

From the detailed documents, price out your labor, based in part on the Cost of Doing Business calculations you made earlier in this chapter, subcontractor costs, materials cost, estimated custom programming effort, margins, fees, and taxes. Don't forget the labor costs of getting to this point. Your minimum quoted price has just been calculated. Now go back and determine the value of what you are providing to the client. It should be greater than your time and materials cost. (If it isn't, you are not adding sufficient value.)

This is the key to Getting Off the Clock—putting a price on the value of your package, not what it costs to produce that package. Value differentiators make your package a better option than your competition in the eyes of the client.

You can now provide the client with a single price for the entire package, noting that modifications to the quoted design are cheerfully allowed at any time. You might also want to break down your package into phases and price each phase, but do so only if your package warrants.

This is a Key Learning: Differentiate yourself by providing exceptional service before, during, and after the sale and implementation. This will turn potential customers into customers and it will turn customers into loyal clients.

Change Orders Are a Good Thing

Change happens, especially in Information Technology, so embrace it and make it work for you. Make each set of changes its own package and provide a single price for it. How many changes make up a set of changes is something that you need to decide as you gain experience with fixed pricing.

Your Expertise

As all good leaders demonstrate, relationships are a requirement for success. Getting Off the Clock is about adding value and building relationships. The core to relationship building is providing value in the eyes of the other person. You need to constantly work on your relationships and provide value. This value and these relationships will be essential to your future business.

Thus far, we have talked about the roles you play as an expert in your niche. In our hypothetical business, you are part of the sales team, customer service team, designer, project manager, general contractor, change coordinator, and problem solver.

As you move up into this level of consulting, away from time and materials work, you end up doing relatively less technical commodity work and relatively more leadership work. You build relationships and partners while gaining clients. You may provide commodity products or services in your package, but people working under your auspices deliver them. You focus on the additional value to the client and you build relationships with business partners to add commodity products and services that you don't do or no longer perform.

Customers vs. Clients

This is a Key Learning: Clients are customers that you have made loyal to your business due to the value you have demonstrated and the relationship you have built with them. Treat every potential customer like a future client.

Always invoice for the full price, and decide whether you will provide "Good Guy Discounts" upon occasion to show your appreciation for your best clients. It is so much less expensive to retain a happy client and have them provide word-of-mouth referrals to their friends than to either find a new customer to turn into a client or have an unhappy client talk to their friends about their dissatisfaction.

Top Computer Consultants Get Paid

Bonnie D. Huval

Bonnie's USA and UK consulting firms especially focus on large custom realtime and near-realtime systems for factory process control, telecom and pharmaceutical manufacturing. She has a long record of successful IT projects for clients that include well known multinationals. She also has active business holdings in residential and commercial real estate, a growing property management firm, and a restaurant. In the past she served on the board of directors for a national USA non-profit, and was among the leaders in pulling the organization away from the financial brink.

Bonnie's consulting firm had people working at WorldCom when that company was spiraling toward bankruptcy. Other firms around hers waited longer and longer for payment, but hers got paid on time and in full. She publishes for small businesses about topics that are essential for survival, yet frequently overlooked. Her presentation about making sure to get paid had a standing room only audience at the 2003 ICCA Conference.

You can reach her through her USA firm Seneschal Incorporated at **www.seneschal.biz**.

If You Bill Them, Will They Pay?

You may think it's obvious that top computer consultants get paid for the value they deliver to clients. But in business, getting paid is not guaranteed. Along the way to excellence, one way or another, consultants learn that some customers need to be encouraged or nudged to keep up with their bills.

A friend who became a computer consultant long before me never made the transition to the top tier, and never learned to deal with customers in ways that would make sure they paid. Twice, he was unable to collect invoices of more than $50,000. A few more times, he left more than $15,000 uncollected.

If you are a top notch computer consultant, you are really delivering a blend of technical expertise and business acumen—and your business sense shows in the way you run your own practice. You don't leave yourself exposed to deadbeats like my friend did. You use the right procedures, contracts and soft skills to get your customers to pay what they owe when it is due.

Basics of Making Sure You Get Paid

Making sure you get paid does not have a simple canned solution. You must integrate knowledge of your customers, behavior that encourages customers to take you seriously, clauses in your contracts and terms, procedures, and enforcement tools to make it happen. Here is a quick outline of how you do it.

You only extend credit to customers when it is appropriate.

Providing goods or services first and then sending an invoice is an extension of credit to your customers. Just like a banker, when the customer may not be willing or able to pay, or when the size of the contract is too large to risk, you should not extend credit.

You bill completely and promptly, and process incoming payments promptly.

You develop and follow good procedures for timekeeping, milestone tracking, invoicing, recording incoming payments and making deposits.

The only freebies you give away are deliberate.

You know exactly what are you selling. You sell only what you intend to sell, and give away only what you intend to give away.

Your contracts set correct limits on what you sell and do. No contract is ever allowed to unreasonably restrain you from doing business with other customers. Your proprietary tools, ideas, procedures, or other trade secrets are protected. You sell license rights instead of ownership, unless you truly intend to sell ownership.

If your most valuable product is intangible, you recognize it, especially when it is what customers regard as your most important offering. If you didn't realize you are selling it, you could inadvertently give it away free of charge!

Your contracts are valid.

You only make deals with people who have legal standing to agree to their side of the contract. If you didn't, you could sign an invalid contract and have no way to make them pay.

Your contracts are well written. Liability and indemnification are appropriate and thorough. Deliverables, acceptance mechanisms and time limits are clearly defined. Invoicing and payment terms and timelines are clear.

Your attorney can probably write adequate clauses for liability and indemnification, but needs your help to understand:

- What you must deliver

- How expenses (especially travel) are to be handled

- What happens if you cannot fulfill your promises because of a dependency on someone else who falls short, or a disaster beyond your control

- How your customer's acceptance and satisfaction are signified

- What warranty you offer and what you are obligated to do if the customer is not satisfied

You collaborate with your attorney to make each contract a good one. After the first in-depth collaboration, brief guidance to your attorney is probably enough for most subsequent contracts.

You have procedures for responding when a customer disputes a bill.

Because your contracts are well written, the reason for any dispute over a bill can be readily pinpointed and resolved to clear your customer's objection. This gets you paid and maintains a good relationship with your customer.

You don't allow customers to age the bills, take undeserved discounts, send payments that are no good, or never pay.

You accept forms of payment that fit the business relationship. Typical forms of payment include: cash, certified or cashier's check, traveler's check, money order, personal or business check, wire transfer, electronic funds transfer, credit card, charge card, debit card, or cyberspace payment service (e.g. Paypal). You know which forms suit your business best.

When you are certain a customer will only take incentive discounts they deserve, you offer incentive discounts to encourage promptness or payment by the method you prefer. My most reliable long term customer gets a discount for paying quickly via electronic funds transfer, as an example.

With customers whose checks might bounce, you require safer forms of payment and tighter terms of sale.

Aging the bills is a term for paying bills at the last moment before you would take an action the customer is unwilling to bear, instead of paying when bills are due. Organizations in a cash flow squeeze need to age their bills in order to survive. Many large companies age their bills even during good times. Your contracts and procedures nip this in the bud.

Before a customer can get very far out of line on payments, you pounce on the problem. You find out why they haven't paid, and either prod them into paying or negotiate with them to establish a payment plan if they truly are not able to pay at the moment.

You have effective ways to make a delinquent customer pay.

Of course you do—this is how you keep customers from aging your bills. Collection agencies and legal action are slow, expensive, combative last resorts that can become a bigger problem than the unpaid bill. You don't let matters deteriorate that far.

When a customer never pays despite being able to, inflicting an intolerable consequence is your best way to wring out the payment. If you do everything else right but cannot impose intolerable consequences, you cannot make your customer pay. This tends to be a matter of business more than law.

For example, the software you deliver may require a license key 30 days after the final payment is due, and you issue the key only after payment is in hand. If you deliver hardware, depending upon federal and state law, a critical hardware item (such as a fuse that is installed, but removable) may be subject to repossession if the bill is not paid.

You are prepared if a customer goes bankrupt or dies.

Solid documentation is part of your normal procedures. If your customer dies unexpectedly, you can produce what the executor of the estate needs to see in order to pay you from the estate.

You know your customers well, so it is exceedingly rare for you to be blindsided by a customer's insolvency. But if your customer does go bankrupt while your bills are outstanding, you are able to prove to the bankruptcy court what you are owed, and whether the debt is secured (with higher priority to get paid) or unsecured.

Basic Yet Essential

None of this is terribly sophisticated. Some of it is even boring to do. But the rewards for taking care of everything on that list are great.

I've had my own business since 1992. Although I had one painful $11,000 learning experience from an unreliable payer, my consulting firm has never resorted to a collections agent or legal action. The only write-off for an uncollectible bill is less than 20% of my unhappy learning experience.

If I could get my firm paid on time even while doing business with WorldCom in its decline, so can you!

Success at Succession

Steve Epner

Steve began his career learning to program in Fortran at the Illinois Institute of Technology in 1965. He was hooked. After receiving a Computer Science degree from Purdue University in 1970, he became a full time computer geek. In 1976, Steve broke out of the world of safe employment and started his own consulting company. Originally called The User Group (because end users should be the most important piece in the IT puzzle), by the early 1990s his company was getting calls about drug rehabilitation.

Through mergers and acquisitions, the company grew and grew. In 2005, Steve sold his interests and flunked retirement. He returned to Purdue and earned a Master of Science from the School of Technology. In 2007, he was appointed the Innovator in Residence at Saint Louis University.

*Steve founded the Independent Computer Consultants Association in 1976 to be able to learn from others in the field. He is still active in promoting the industry, teaching future leaders and staying engaged. Steve can be reached at **sepner@slu.edu**.*

Getting Ready for the Rest of Your Life

I refuse to use the "R" word. There are so many other "r" words that work. This is a time in my life when I am reinventing myself. It is a time of revision and reinvigoration. I am renewed. I am everything but *retired*.

This chapter is to help you prepare yourself and your business for the next stage of your life. It is a positive. It is all about getting ready and doing it right.

You can find many books on the fiscal planning that is necessary. They will tell you how to invest your money and set yourself up for an easy lifestyle. Others will tell you how to sell or structure a business. But most of them do not understand the world of consulting or the individual consultant who owns a "job." As a matter of fact, most writers will tell you that individual consulting practices cannot be sold.

Here, we are talking about the reality of what it will take and the human side of preparation. What are the steps you need to take to prepare yourself and your company? We are focused on the part most of the literature ignores.

Why Bother About Succession?

Why do you need to plan for succession? It is easy to think, "I am too young to worry about retiring." That single thought occurs in business owners from their early 30s to their later 70s. Old age is always 15 years ahead of us. We feel like we can, and will, keep going forever.

In the world of technical consulting, it is also easy to say, "Everyone knows you cannot sell a consulting business. Anyway, I am going to have to work until I die." That is depressing. The good news is that it need not be that way.

Over the years I have seen every type of consulting business you can imagine. There are one person shops who are really employees, just not on payroll. Others have built lifestyle practices that support travel or just very comfortable living. There are small firms (2 to 10 employees or sub-contractors), and there are full blown businesses. Here, I am focused on the first three. The full blown business is capable of taking care of itself. There are many advisors who can help them.

For the individual or small firm, it is important to start by understanding what can be sold. Most business people want to purchase assets. These may include existing contracts, people, and even "good will." The problem is understanding how an outsider values these assets.

As a business looking at a transition, prepare yourself for the question, "Why should I pay $X for your firm when I can start my own firm and not pay you a cent?"

The answer is that you are selling them time. If they want to do it themselves, it will take the same number of years you needed to have a comfortable business. They are buying your history, introductions to your network, your satisfied clients, your contractors and employees who do such a good job that you keep getting repeat business. They are buying all that you built—and it can be worth a great deal.

If you have software, publications, annuity revenue streams, or other income producing assets, those increase the value of your business. Now you just have to find someone who is willing to pay a fair price to take over the operation. Unlike many other businesses, you will probably have to take your buyout over time. That is a fact of life in this field. With proper planning, it can be very lucrative, set you up for a wonderful future, and allow you to stay engaged if you wish.

So, it is possible to have a life after a consulting business. All it takes is a bit of planning and a realistic attitude.

The truth is that most of us do not want to face the inevitable. We are getting older. We are going to lose our edge and perspective. We are not going to be able to keep up the pace that has made us successful.

Down the road, there will be a transition. It will either be well planned and executed, or occur as an emergency. Emergencies usually involve a sudden loss through an accident, health problem, or an unexpected demise. (I hate the word *death* almost as much as I hate the word *retirement*.)

Unexpected occurrences like sudden changes in the business environment, government regulation and the marketplace may force an unplanned succession. None of us can control if or when there might be an emergency, so we all must plan for the eventualities as early as possible.

Six Reasons to Plan for Succession

1. It Is Good Business

I have proven that even a small consulting business can be sold and a transition made to younger management. One of your responsibilities to your family, employees and clients is the long term success of the company. You know how important it is to prepare for the future. Each of us must make sure the company is able to provide for ourselves and our families in case anything happens to us (or a key employee, if you have one).

2. It Protects the Company

The company can survive into the future only if succession has been planned and prepared in advance. Very few companies take the time to be ready for a personnel disaster. As leaders of our companies, we need to highlight the need and, more importantly, do something about it. Building depth and experience is in our selfish best interest. It can also be a selling tool in the marketplace. New potential clients can be more secure knowing there is a plan.

3. It Creates Opportunity for Younger Consultants

The future of every company is in its younger employees or potential owners. Preparing for succession of the older guys and gals (older only because it takes time to gain experience and develop management skills) encourages us to recruit, train, and mentor the up and coming young people who will run the company in the future.

Mentoring is the way we instill the positive values of our companies' culture, history and mission in the next generation. Growth of the business does not change who we are, only who is doing what.

For many individual consultants, this is the most difficult part. Our sense of personal identity is often closely tied to the work we do. We never wanted to have employees and have resisted the urge and opportunity at every juncture.

Although we may not want to build a large organization, it is possible to find someone who wants to be able to buy your company over time. They may want to build it into a larger firm, but leave that to them. Just find the right person, make the transition and enjoy the buyout.

4. It Creates Continuity

Sudden change causes discontinuity. Often outsiders are brought in to complete any work. There may be arguments about who bears the cost of the new contractors, their training, and any extra time necessary to come up to speed. These people may not understand (or even care) what made the company successful. Good succession planning and execution provides continuity for our clients and families. The right program also ensures the transfer of relationships and networks to keep the company strong and growing.

5. It Allows Successful Exits

We know that nothing is forever. Everyone will leave their job at some point. It may be planned or sudden. But in one way or another, there will be a change.

Too many owners are unable to move on with their lives. They are stuck in the past and cannot seem to get ready for the future. Do not believe the negative voices that would have you believe there are no choices.

You can leave behind a positive legacy while going through the door to a productive (by your definition) future.

Sometimes we hide our own vulnerability from ourselves. We do not want to deal with changes that are potentially painful. Let's face it, many changes in smaller companies (and large ones too) occur due to sickness, tragic accidents and death. Not a very positive triplet.

There are other reasons as well. At the top of the list are natural moves. There are many people who decide to move cities for personal reasons all of the time. A spouse may get a better job offer. Elderly parents may need care and be unable relocate themselves. Better climates attract many and some just move for the heck of it. In each case a transition will occur.

In some cases, people will change their minds. A promise to work until 70 may not make it past a 65th birthday. Maybe it is a sudden recognition of one's own mortality. As people age, priorities change. Time becomes a valuable commodity and we change plans to take advantage of what is left.

Finally, stuff happens. In some cases, long term employees (if you already have them) are dismissed for a wide variety of reasons (not all of them positive). Jealousies, unintentional slights, changes in reporting relationships, and many other causes are blamed for forcing people to make abrupt changes. Any of these will disrupt an organization that is not ready.

Depending on circumstances, there may be little or no time to prepare. This is where advanced planning proves its worth. By accepting that change will happen, it is possible to be ready for it without fear, finger pointing or other negative behavior which would make the transition tougher and less successful.

6. Small Consulting Businesses are Different

While most succession planning is the same for any type of organization, small consulting businesses have special issues. These must be addressed early in the process or they defeat all planning.

As the owner, it will also be important to be honest with yourself and your potential successors. First, you may not be very good at taking orders from any of them. Second, they may not really be capable of running the company. Third, your favorite friend may not be the best choice and selecting someone else may cause more heartache then you are willing to accept.

Counselors, psychologists and other professions may be needed to help you get through the process. It can be done and it will only hurt a little. Not doing it can ultimately cause many people much more pain.

When is the Best Time to Start?

It is never too early. That is the easy answer. There is an old saying, "Life is what happens while you are making other plans."

Now, the facts. Your time frame depends on many different issues. While it is always best to be ready far in advance, in reality most of us wait until the last minute to start on projects that are difficult, uncomfortable, outside our comfort zone, or force us to admit to our own mortality.

For a small business, it is never too early to get started. You need to find another person like you, willing to work crazy hours, put up with crazy clients, and be willing to share money with you while buying the company.

We all like to believe we have something special that has allowed us to be successful. Our starting time is related to how long we believe it will take to find and train a person so they can do our job almost as well as we can do it ourselves. If training someone in your specialty will only take a week, then you probably have nothing to worry about.

More likely, it will take a year or more. One year is possible only if there is a key employee that is just about ready without any outside help. For most organizations, two years is a reasonable minimum.

From my experience, it can take much longer. Most timelines are extended because the first (and often the second) chosen successors fail. (I needed three chances.) We are just not good at picking the right people. Few owner/consultants have the experience to objectively pick the right person the first time.

Gut feel does not always work. Egos can get in the way. Personal feelings about individuals can affect judgment. Give yourself time to make mistakes—you are only human.

How Do I Identify Successors?

This is not an easy question. One process is to find a clone that can just move in and keep things going as they are. Another view is to find a different kind of person who will see the opportunities that you may not have been willing to chase. That person in a two year transition can help build a firm that has greater value and can afford to pay a decent sum over some period of time to make the next phase of your life sweet and easy.

Some consultants use this approach to build the company they always wanted, but have been afraid to build on their own. They use the desire of another person wanting their business to raise some capital and invest in growth. You may even be able to keep an ownership position (after the sale/transfer is finalized) that pays greater dividends in addition to the buyout.

Whichever path you select, establish a time frame within which to complete the training and relationship activities. How soon should the training be done? Are there any predetermined dates (like a planned retirement) that must be met? How long will the planned activities take? What order should they be accomplished in? This may be the most important project you undertake. Give it the best planning you can.

Make sure to plan for frequent evaluations. It is important to react quickly if there is any indication that your selection is not working. There may be a personality conflict or there just may not be sufficient horsepower available. In either case, the company should not waste time, energy or resources trying to fit a square peg in a round hole.

Building a Plan

History has taught us that nothing will go smoothly or right on time, so we must plan for contingencies. Still, try to stay ahead of the game. The more buffer space you can build, the more choices you will have when things get tight.

Be realistic in your planning. Work backwards from the worst possible date to see what you might need to do if Uncle Murphy (Murphy's laws) sits on your shoulder. Then start the process as soon as possible. It is never too early.

For each step, write out a plan to complete the required training or turnover. This may include formal outside training. It may be "shadow" time so your successor can see how you currently run the business. Self study and practice are also good ways to build new skills.

The only way to make sure the learning is working is to provide opportunities for real action. Over the training period, the selected successor needs to be given more and more responsibility and **must** be allowed to fail. They need to know they will survive a few bumps. They need opportunities to test their capabilities.

After each such test, they need to be able to debrief with you. This is the way to hone and perfect their skills.

After you have identified the prospects and established the plan, you must work to make it successful. Any plan can succeed or fail. You need to establish clear responsibilities for it to work.

Any potential buyer/successor must know that success is not guaranteed. You do not want someone who can just get by; you want to build a **key** employee. They are expected to do more.

It is also important for them to have some of their own assets at risk. Maybe they work for a smaller salary in return for training. Maybe they have to put up an irrevocable down payment. The specifics can be negotiated. It is necessary for them to have "skin in the game" so they will work as hard as you do to make the transition a success.

You are looking for people who are capable of running the business. People who will:

- take responsibility

- make decisions, and

- lead.

Anything less and they can stay where they were. You do not want them to become the next owner.

Pulling the Trigger

Once you are committed to making the change, stick to your timetable. Few things are worse than starting something and never finishing it. You can destroy the opportunity to be able to transition and all of the positive benefits that entails.

Plus, as people get used to the idea of you leaving, that is the time to do it. Even if you only postpone it, your credibility will be diminished. Others who are making plans based on your statements can become disenchanted and leave. At the very least, they will not believe you the next time you announce a major date for anything.

The last two items of advice on this topic are **do not turn back** and **do not interfere**. There will always be Chicken Littles who will think the sky is falling just because you are not there. Others will disagree with a decision made by the new owner and hope you will override it. Any of these actions will most certainly hurt your successor's credibility and ability to manage the business.

One of the best things you can do is take a long vacation right after turning over the reins. (My wife and I went to Australia and New Zealand for a month.) That will give each of you time to get used to the new environment. Then accept special projects, but stay out of the day-to-day activities of the company for at least six months. Your replacement deserves time to establish themselves in their new position.

Of course, if there is a real emergency and your contacts, calm demeanor, management capability, business knowledge or other positive traits are needed, do respond. To the extent possible, do all of your work as a subordinate of the new chief. It may be difficult, but it will improve the transition.

Wrapping Up

At this point, it is up to you. We all know that nothing is forever and that includes us. Right now is the time to consider the options, plan for the future and begin execution of that plan.

As a business leader, being surprised by the inevitable is just plain stupid. A lack of foresight in this one area can destroy everything you have built. Do not risk it.

Take charge of the situation. Commit to yourself, your family and your associates. You can make it happen.

The future may be unknown, but only a fool ignores it. Each of us has the experience and vision to see what is coming—at least at the "big picture" level. Do not wait for an emergency to force your hand. Continue to lead. That is what got you to where you are.

Let me leave you with a wish of good luck and success. It is not that hard. Just remember three things:

You can plan.

You can prepare.

You can leave a legacy.

Index

About ICCA

The Independent Computer Consultants Association is a professional community of business information technology computer consultants. Since 1976, ICCA members are the experts clients rely on for independent, unbiased, and ethical consulting relationships providing business analysis, strategic planning, IT infrastructure support, training, web site / application, software development, and digital media consulting.

ICCA provides a growing number of member benefits, supported by our Local Chapters, including

- Special Interest Groups focused on specific consulting topics

- Education and Training Webinars

- Discounts off books, office equipment and rental car companies

- Web Site including Discussion Boards and Article Library

- Our Annual National Conferences

Student, individual and company memberships are available. All members pledge to adhere to the ICCA Code of Ethics.

Code of Ethics

Below are the ethical standards that the ICCA upheld as essential not only for its members but for the computer consulting industry as a whole.

- Consultants will be honest and not knowingly misrepresent facts.

- Consultants will install and use only properly licensed software on their systems as well as the clients' systems.

- Consultants will divulge any potential conflicts of interest prior to accepting the contract or as soon as possible after the conflict is discovered.

- Consultants will only represent opinions as independent if they are free from subordinated judgment and there is no undisclosed interest in the outcome of the client's decision.

- Consultants will ensure that to the best of their knowledge they can complete the project in a professional manner both in terms of skill and time.

- Consultants will keep the client informed of any matters relating to the contract even if the information is unfavorable, or may jeopardize the contract.

- Consultants will safeguard any confidential information or documents entrusted to them and not divulge any confidential information without the consent of the client.

- Consultants will not take advantage of proprietary information obtained from the client.

- Consultants will not engage in contracts that are in violation of the law or that might reasonably be used by client to violate the law.

ICCA member firms, their principals and employees will uphold the principles of the ICCA and not commit acts discreditable to the ICCA.

www.ingramcontent.com/pod-product-compliance
Lightning Source LLC
Chambersburg PA
CBHW051248050326
40689CB00007B/1118